Comfort for Christians

Martha Richards (handwritten)

ARTHUR W. PINK

Calvainist Scotland (handwritten)

With
DEVOTIONAL AIDS
Including
"Daily Bread": A Calendar for Reading
through the Bible in a Year, with Directions,
by Robert Murray M'Cheyne
and
"My Prayer Requests and God's Answers":
a Suggested *Register of Petitions*

Large Print Edition

Baker Book House
Grand Rapids, Michigan

ISBN 0-8010-6999-8

CONTENTS

INTRODUCTION

The work to which the servant of Christ is called is many-sided. Not only is he to preach the Gospel to the unsaved, to feed God's people with knowledge and understanding (Jer. 3:15), and to take up the stumbling stone out of their way (Is. 57:14), but he is also charged to "cry aloud, spare not, lift up thy voice like a trumpet, and show My people their transgression" (Is. 58:1 and cf. I Tim. 4:2). Yet another important part of his commission is stated thus: "Comfort ye, comfort ye My people, saith your God" (Is. 40:1).

What an honorable title, "My people"! What an assuring relationship, "your God"! What a pleasant task, "comfort ye My people"! A threefold reason may be suggested for the duplicating of the charge. First, believers sometimes refuse to be comforted (Ps. 77:2) and the consolation needs to be repeated. A second reason is to impress more emphatically on the preacher's heart that he need not be sparing in administering cheer. A third reason is to assure us how heartily desirous God himself is that His people be of good cheer (Phil. 4:4).

God has a "people," the objects of His special favor: a company whom He has taken into such intimate relationship with Himself that He calls them "My people." Often they are disconsolate because of their natural corruptions, the temptations of Satan, the cruel treatment of the world, the low state of Christ's cause on earth. The "God of all comfort" (II Cor. 1:3) is very tender toward them, and it is His revealed will that His servants should bind up the broken-hearted and pour the balm of Gilead into their wounds. What cause we have to exclaim "Who is a God like unto

5

Thee"! (Micah 7:18), who has provided for the comfort of those who were rebels against His government and transgressors of His Law.

May it please Him to use His Word as expounded in this book to speak peace to afflicted souls today, and the glory shall be His alone.

A. W. Pink, 1952

1

NO CONDEMNATION

"There is therefore now no condemnation to them which are in Christ Jesus" (ROMANS 8:1).

"There is therefore now no condemnation." The eighth chapter of the epistle to the Romans concludes the first section of that wonderful epistle. Its opening word "therefore" ("There is" is in italics because supplied by the translators) may be viewed in a twofold way. First, it culminates the preceding discussion. Because Christ has been set forth "a propitiation through faith in His blood" (3:25); because He was "delivered for our offences and raised again for our justification" (4:25); because by the obedience of the One the many (believers of all ages) are "made righteous," constituted so, legally, (5:19); because believers have "died (judicially) to sin" (6:2); because they have "died" to the condemning power of the law (7:4); there is "therefore now NO CONDEMNATION."

But not only is the "therefore" to be viewed as a conclusion drawn from the whole of the previous discussion, it is also to be considered as having a close relation to what *immediately* precedes. In the second half of Romans 7 the apostle had described the painful and ceaseless conflict waged between the two antagonistic natures in one who has been born again, illustrating this by a reference to his own personal experiences as a Christian. Having portrayed with a master pen (himself sitting for the picture) the spiritual struggles of the child of God, the apostle now proceeds to direct attention to the Divine consolation for a condition so distressing and humiliating. The transition from the despondent tone of the seventh chapter to the triumphant language of the eighth ap-

7

pears startling and abrupt, yet it is quite logical and natural. If it is true that to the saints of God belongs the conflict of sin and death, under whose effects they mourn, equally true is it that their deliverance from the curse and the corresponding condemnation is a victory in which they rejoice. A very striking contrast is thus set forth. In the second half of Romans 7 the apostle discusses the power of sin that operates in believers as long as they are in the world; in the opening verses of chapter eight, he speaks of the guilt of sin from which they are completely delivered the moment they are united to the Savior by faith. Hence in 7:24 the apostle asks "Who shall deliver me" from the power of sin; but in 8:2 he says, "hath made me free," i.e. has delivered me from the guilt of sin.

"There is therefore now no condemnation." It is not here a question of our heart condemning us (as in I John 3:21), nor of our finding nothing within worthy of condemnation; instead, it is the far more blessed fact that God condemns not the one who has trusted in Christ for the saving of his soul. We need to distinguish sharply between objective and subjective truth; between that which is judicial and that which is experiential; otherwise, we shall fail to draw from such Scriptures as the one now before us the comfort and peace they are designed to convey. There is no condemnation to them who are in Christ Jesus. "In Christ" is the believer's position before God, not his condition in the flesh. "In Adam" I was condemned (Rom. 5:12), but "in Christ" I am forever freed from all condemnation.

"There is therefore now no condemnation." The qualifying "now" implies there was a time when Christians, before they believed, were under condemnation. This was before they died with Christ, died judicially (Gal. 2:20) under the penalty of God's righteous law. This "now" distinguishes between two states or conditions. By nature we were "under the (sentence of) law," but now as believers we are "under grace" (Rom. 6:14). By nature we were "children of wrath" (Eph. 2:2), but now we are "accepted in the Beloved" (Eph. 1:6). Under the first covenant we were "in Adam" (I Cor. 15:22), but now we are "in Christ" (Rom. 8:1). As believers in Christ we have everlasting life, and because of this we "shall not come into condemnation."

Condemnation is a word of tremendous import, and the better we understand it the more we shall appreciate the wondrous grace that has delivered us from its power. In the halls of a human court this is a term which falls with fearful knell on the ear of the convicted criminal and fills the spectators with sadness and horror. But in the court of Divine Justice it is vested with a meaning and content infinitely more solemn and awe-inspiring. To that Court every member of Adam's fallen race is cited. "Conceived in sin, and shapen in iniquity" each one enters this world under arrest; an indicted criminal, a rebel manacled. How, then, is it possible for such a one to escape the execution of the dread sentence? There is only one way, and that is by the removal from us of that which called forth the sentence, namely, sin. Let guilt be removed and there can be "no condemnation."

Has guilt really been removed from the sinner who believes? Let the following Scriptures answer: "As far as the east is from the west so far hath he removed our transgressions from us" (Ps. 103:12). "I, even I, am he that blotteth out thy transgressions" (Is. 43:25). "Thou hast cast all my sins behind thy back" (Is. 38:17). "Their sins and iniquities will I remember no more" (Heb. 10:17).

But how could guilt be removed? Only by its being transferred. Divine holiness could not ignore it; but Divine grace could and did transfer it. The sins of believers were transferred to Christ: "The Lord hath laid on him the iniquity of us all" (Is. 53:6). "For he hath made him to be sin for us" (II Cor. 5:21).

"There is therefore now no condemnation." The "no" is

emphatic. It signifies there is no condemnation whatsoever. No condemnation from the law, or on account of inward corruption, or because Satan can substantiate a charge against me; there is none from any source or for any cause at all. "No condemnation" means that none at all is or ever will be possible. There is no condemnation because there is no accusation (see 8:33), and there can be no accusation because there is no imputation of sin (see 4:8).

"There is therefore now no condemnation to them which are in Christ Jesus." When discussing the conflict between the two natures in the believer, the apostle had in the previous chapter spoken of himself in his own person, in order to show that the highest attainments in grace do not exempt one from the internal warfare that he there describes. But here in 8:1 the apostle changes the number. He does not say, There is no condemnation to me, but "to them which are in Christ Jesus." This was most gracious of the Holy Spirit. Had the apostle spoken here in the singular number, we should have reasoned that such a blessed exemption was well suited to this honored servant of God who enjoyed such wondrous privileges; but could not apply to *us*. The Spirit of God, therefore, moved the apostle to employ the plural number here, to show that "no condemnation" is true of *all* in Christ Jesus.

"There is therefore now no condemnation to them which are in Christ Jesus." To be in Christ Jesus is to be perfectly identified with Him in the judicial reckonings and dealings of God; and it is also to be one with him in vital union by faith. Immunity from condemnation does not depend in **any** way on our "walk," but solely on our being "in Christ." "The believer is in Christ as Noah was enclosed within the ark, with the heavens darkening above him, and the waters heaving beneath him, yet not a drop of the flood penetrating his vessel, not a blast of the storm disturbing the serenity of his spirit. The believer is in Christ as Jacob was in the garment of the elder brother when Isaac kissed and blessed him. He is in Christ as the poor homicide was within the city of refuge when pursued by the avenger of blood, but who could not overtake and slay him" (Octavius Winslow, 1857) . And because he is "in Christ" there is, therefore, no condemnation for him. Hallelujah!

2

THE CHRISTIAN'S ASSURANCE

"And we know that all things work together for good to them that love God, to them who are the called according to His purpose" (ROMANS 8:28).

How many of God's children through the centuries have drawn strength and comfort from this blessed verse. In the midst of trials, perplexities, and persecutions, this has been a rock beneath their feet. Though to outward sight things seemed to work against their good, though to carnal reason things appeared to be working for their ill, nevertheless, faith knew it was far otherwise. And how great the loss to those who failed to rest in this inspired declaration: what unnecessary fears and doubtings were the consequence.

"All things work together." The first thought occurring to us is this: What a glorious Being is our God, who is able to make all things so work! What a frightful amount of evil is in constant motion. What an almost infinite number of creatures there are in the world. What an incalculable quantity of opposing self-interests are at work. What a vast army of rebels are fighting against God. What hosts of superhuman creatures are ever opposing the Lord. And yet, high above all, is GOD, in undisturbed calm, complete master of the situation. There, from the throne of His exalted majesty, He works all things after the counsel of His own will (Eph. 1:11). Stand in awe, then, before this One in whose sight "all nations are as nothing; and they are counted as less than nothing, and vanity" (Is. 40:17). Bow in adoration before this "high and lofty One that inhabiteth eternity" (Is. 57:15). Lift high your praise to Him who from the direst evil can bring forth the greatest good.

12

"All things work." In nature there is no such thing as a vacuum, neither is there a creature of God that fails to serve its designed purpose. Nothing is idle. Everything is energized by God to fulfill its intended mission. All things are laboring toward the grand end of their Creator's pleasure; all are moved at His imperative bidding.

"All things work together." They not only operate, they cooperate; they all act in perfect concert, though none but the anointed ear can catch the strains of their harmony. All things work together, not singly but conjointly, as attending causes and mutual helps. That is why afflictions seldom come one at a time. Cloud rises on cloud, storm on storm. As with Job, one messenger of woe is quickly succeeded by another, burdened with tidings of yet heavier sorrow. Nevertheless, even here faith may trace both the wisdom and love of God. It is the compounding of the ingredients in the recipe that constitutes its beneficent value. So with God: His dispensations not only "work," but they "work together." So recognized the sweet singer of Israel: "He drew me out of many waters" (Ps. 18:16) .

"All things work together for good to," etc. These words teach believers that no matter what the number nor how overwhelming the character of adverse circumstances, they are all helping to lead them into the possession of their inheritance in heaven. How wonderful the providence of God is in overruling the most disorderly things; and in turning to our good things that in themselves are most pernicious! We marvel at His mighty power that holds the heavenly bodies in their orbits and at the continually recurring seasons and the renewal of the earth. But this is not nearly so marvelous as His bringing good out of evil in all the complicated occurrences of human life, and making even the power and malice of Satan's destructive works to minister good for His children.

"All things work together for good." This must be so for

three reasons. First, because all things are under the absolute control of the Governor of the universe. Second, because God desires our good, and nothing but our good. Third, because even Satan himself cannot touch a hair of our heads without God's permission, and then only for our further good. Not all things are good in themselves or in their tendencies; but God makes all things work for our good. Nothing enters our life by blind chance, nor are there any accidents. Everything is being moved by God with this end in view: our good. The subservience of everything to God's eternal purpose works blessing to those marked out for conformity to the image of the Firstborn. All suffering, sorrow, and loss are used by our Father to minister to the benefit of His elect.

"To them that love God." This is the grand distinguishing feature of every true Christian. The reverse marks all the unregenerate. The saints are those who love God. Their creeds may differ in minor details, their ecclesiastical relations may vary in outward form, their gifts and graces may be very unequal; yet, in this particular there is an essential unity. They all believe in Christ, they all love God. They love Him for the gift of the Savior; they love Him as a Father in whom they may confide; they love Him for His personal excellencies, His holiness, wisdom, and faithfulness. They love Him for His conduct: for what He withholds and for what He grants; for what He rebukes and for what He approves. They love Him even for the rod that disciplines, knowing that He does all things well. There is nothing in God and there is nothing from God for which the saints do not love Him. And of this they are all assured, "We love Him because He first loved us."

"To them that love God." But, alas, how little I love God! I so frequently mourn my lack of love, and chide myself for the coldness of my heart. Yes, there is so much love of self and love of the world that sometimes I seriously question if I have any real love for God at all. But is not my very desire to love God a good symptom? Is not my very grief that I love Him so little a sure evidence that I do not hate Him? The presence of a hard and ungrateful heart has been mourned over by the saints of all ages. "Love to God is a heavenly aspiration, that is ever kept in check by the drag and restraint of an earthly nature; and from which we shall not be unbound till the soul has made its escape from the vile body, and cleared its unfettered way to the realm of light and liberty" (Dr. Chalmers).

"Who are called." The word "called" in the New Testament Epistles is never applied to those who are recipients of a mere external invitation of the Gospel. The term always signifies an inward and effectual call. It was a call over which we had no control, either in originating or frustrating it. So in Rom. 1:6, 7 and many other passages: "Among whom are ye also the called of Jesus Christ: to all that be in Rome, beloved of God, called saints." Has this call reached *you*, my reader? Ministers have called you, the Gospel has called you, conscience has called you; but has the Holy Spirit called you with an inward and irresistible call? Have you been spiritually called from darkness to light, from death to life, from the world to Christ, from self to God? It is a matter of the greatest moment that you should know whether you have been truly called of God. Has, then, the thrilling, life-giving music of that call sounded and reverberated through all the chambers of your soul? But how may I be sure that I have received such a call? There is one thing right here in our text which should enable you to tell. They who have been efficaciously called, love God. Instead of hating Him, they now esteem Him; instead of fleeing from Him in terror, they now seek Him; instead of not caring whether their conduct honors or dishonors Him, their deepest desire now is to please and glorify Him.

"According to His purpose." The call is not according to

the merits of men, but according to the Divine purpose: "Who hath saved us, and called us with an holy calling, not according to our works, but according to his own purpose and grace, which was given us in Christ Jesus before the world began" (II Tim. 1:9). The design of the Holy Spirit in bringing in this last clause is to show that the reason some men love God and others do not is to be attributed solely to the sovereignty of God: it is not for anything in themselves, but due alone to His distinguishing grace.

There is also a practical value in this last clause. The doctrines of grace are intended for a further purpose than that of making up a creed. One main design of them is to move the affections; especially to reawaken that affection which is wholly insufficient in the heart oppressed with fears or weighed down with cares: the love of God. For this love to flow perennially from our hearts there must be a constant recurring to that which inspired it and is calculated to increase it, just as to rekindle your admiration of a beautiful scene or picture you would return again to gaze at it. This principle accounts for the stress in Scripture on keeping the truths we believe in our memory: "By which also ye are saved, if ye keep in memory what I preached unto you" (I Cor. 15:2). "I stir up your pure minds by way of remembrance," said the apostle (II Pet. 3:1). "Do this in remembrance of me" said the Savior. It is, then, by going back in memory to that hour when, despite our wretchedness and utter unworthiness, God called us, that our affection will be kept fresh. It is by recalling the wondrous grace that then reached out to a hell-deserving sinner and snatched you as a brand from the burning, that your heart will be drawn out in adoring gratitude. And it is by discovering that due alone to the sovereign and eternal "purpose" of God you were called when so many others are passed by, that your love for Him will be deepened.

Returning to the opening words of our text, we find the apostle (voicing the normal experience of the saints) declares, "We know that all things work together for good." It is something more than a speculative belief. That all things work together for good is even more than a fervent desire. It is not that we merely hope all things will so work, but that we are fully assured all things do so work. The knowledge here spoken of is spiritual, not intellectual. It is a knowledge rooted in our hearts that produces confidence in the truth of it. It is the knowledge of faith that receives everything from the benevolent hand of Infinite Wisdom. It is true that we do not derive much comfort from this knowledge when out of fellowship with God. Nor will it sustain us when faith is not in operation. But when we are in communion with the Lord, when in our weakness we lean hard on Him, then is this blessed assurance ours: "Thou wilt keep him in perfect peace, whose mind is stayed on Thee: because he trusteth in Thee" (Is. 26:3).

A striking exemplification of our text is supplied by the history of Jacob, a man whom in several respects each of us closely resembles. Heavy and dark was the cloud that settled on him. Severe was the test, and fearful the trembling of his faith. His feet were almost gone. Hear his mournful complaint: "And Jacob their father said unto them, Me have ye bereaved of my children: Joseph is not, and Simeon is not, and ye will take Benjamin away: all these things are against me" (Gen. 42:36). And yet those circumstances that to the dim eye of his faith wore so somber a hue, were at that very moment developing and perfecting the events that were to shed around the evening of his life a glorious and cloudless sunset. All things were working together for his good! And so, troubled soul, the "much tribulation" will soon be over. And as you enter the "kingdom of God" you shall then see no longer "through a glass darkly," but in the unshadowed sunlight of the Divine presence, that "all things" did "work together" for your personal and eternal good.

3

SUFFERINGS COMPENSATED

"For I reckon that the sufferings of this present time are not worthy to be compared with the glory which shall be revealed in us" (ROMANS 8:18).

Ah, says someone, that must have been written by a man who was a stranger to suffering, or by one acquainted with nothing more trying than the milder irritations of life. Not so. These words were penned under the direction of the Holy Spirit by one who drank deeply of sorrow's cup, indeed by one who suffered afflictions in their acutest forms. Hear his own testimony: "Of the Jews five times received I forty stripes save one. Thrice was I beaten with rods, once was I stoned, thrice I suffered shipwreck, a night and a day I have been in the deep; in journeyings often, in perils of robbers, in perils of mine own countrymen, in perils by the heathen, in perils in the city, in perils in the wilderness, in perils in the sea, in perils among false brethren; in weariness and painfulness, in watchings often, in hunger and thirst, in fastings often, in cold and nakedness" (II Cor. 11:24-27).

"For I reckon that the sufferings of this present time are not worthy to be compared with the glory which shall be revealed in us." This, then, was the settled conviction not of one of "fortune's favorites," not of one who found life's journey a carpeted pathway bordered with roses, but, instead, of one who was hated by his kinsmen, who was many times beaten black and blue, who knew what it was to be deprived not only of the comforts but the bare necessities of life. How, then, shall we account for his cheery optimism? What was the secret of his elevation over his troubles and trials?

The first thing with which the sorely-tried apostle comforted himself was that the sufferings of the Christian are but of brief duration, limited to "this present time." This is in sharp and solemn contrast to the sufferings of the Christ-rejector. His sufferings will be eternal, torment forever in the Lake of Fire. But far different is it for the believer. His sufferings are restricted to this life on earth, that is compared to a flower that comes forth and is cut down, or to a shadow that flees and continues not. A few short years at most, and we shall pass from this vale of tears into that blissful country where groans and sighs are never heard.

Second, the apostle looked forward with the eye of faith to "the glory." To Paul "the glory" was something more than a beautiful dream. It was a practical reality, exerting a powerful influence on him, consoling him in the most trying hours of adversity. This is one of the real tests of faith. The Christian has a solid support in the time of affliction that the unbeliever has not. The child of God knows that in his Father's presence there is "fulness of joy," and that at His right hand there are "pleasures forever more." And faith appropriates them and lives in their comforting cheer. Just as the Israelites in the wilderness were encouraged by a sight of what awaited them in the promised land (Num. 13:23, 26) , so the one who today walks by faith and not by sight contemplates that which eye has not seen, nor ear heard, but which God by His Holy Spirit has revealed to us (I Cor. 2:9, 10) .

Third, the apostle rejoiced in "the glory which should be revealed in us." We are not yet capable of understanding all that this means. But more than a hint has been given us. There will be:

1. The "glory" of a perfect body. In that day this corruption shall have put on incorruption, and this mortal, immortality. That which was sown in dishonor shall be raised in glory, and that which was sown in weakness shall be raised in power. As we have borne the image of the earthly, we shall bear the image of the heavenly (I Cor. 15:49) .

The content of these expressions is summarized and amplified in Phil. 3:20, 21: "For our conversation is in heaven; from whence also we look for the Saviour, the Lord Jesus Christ: Who shall change our vile body, that it may be fashioned like unto His glorious body, according to the working whereby He is able even to subdue all things unto Himself."

2. There will be the glory of a transformed mind. "For now we see through a glass darkly; but then face to face: now I know in part; but then shall I know even as also I am known" (I Cor. 13:12). O what an orb of intellectual light each glorified mind will be! What range of light it will encompass! What capability of understanding it will enjoy! Then all mysteries will be unraveled, all problems solved, all discrepencies reconciled. Then each truth of God's revelation, each event of His providence, each decision of His government, will stand more transparent and resplendent than the sun itself. Do you in your present quest for spiritual knowledge mourn the darkness of your mind, the weakness of your memory, the limitations of your intellectual faculties? Then rejoice in hope of the glory that is to be revealed in you; when all your intellectual powers shall be renewed, developed, perfected, so that you will know even as you are known.

3. Best of all, there will be the glory of perfect holiness. God's work of grace in us will then be completed. He has promised to "perfect that which concerneth us" (Ps. 138:8). Then will be the consummation of purity. We have been predestinated to be "conformed to the image of His Son" (Rom. 8:29). and when we shall see Him, "we shall be like him" (I John 3:2). Then our minds will be no more defiled by evil imaginations, our consciences no more weighed down by guilt, our affections no more ensnared by unworthy objects.

What a marvelous prospect this is! A "glory" to be revealed in me who now can scarcely reflect a solitary ray of light! In me—so wayward, so unworthy, so sinful; living so little in communion with Him who is the Father of lights! Can it be that in me this glory will be revealed? So affirms the infallible Word of God. If I am a child of light (through being "in Him" who is the radiance of the Father's glory), even though I now dwell amid the world's dark shades, one day I shall outshine the brightness of the firmament. And when the Lord Jesus returns to this earth He shall "be admired in all them that believe" (II Thess. 1:10).

Finally, the apostle here weighed the "sufferings" of this present time over against the "glory" that will be revealed in us, and as he did so he declared that the one is "not worthy to be compared" with the other. The one is earthly, the other is heavenly. The one is transient, the other eternal. As, then, there is no proportion between the finite and the infinite, so there is no comparison between the sufferings of earth and the glory of heaven.

One second of glory will outweigh a lifetime of suffering. What are years of toil, sickness, battling with poverty, sorrow in any or every form, when compared with the glory of Immanuel's land! One drink from the river of pleasure at God's right hand, one breath of Paradise, one hour amid the blood-washed around the throne, will more than compensate for all the tears and groans of earth. "For I reckon that the sufferings of this present time are not worthy to be compared with the glory which shall be revealed in us." May the Holy Spirit enable both writer and reader to lay hold of this with appropriating faith and live in the present possession and enjoyment of it to the praise of the glory of Divine grace.

4

THE GREAT GIVER

"He that spared not His own Son, but delivered Him up for us all, how shall He not with Him also freely give us all things?" (ROMANS 8:32).

The above verse supplies us with an instance of Divine logic. It contains a conclusion drawn from the premise that since God delivered up Christ for all His people, therefore everything else that is needed by them is sure to be given. There are many examples in Holy Writ of such Divine logic. "If God so clothe the grass of the field, which today is and tomorrow is cast into the oven, shall he not much more clothe you?" (Mt. 6:30). "If when we were enemies we were reconciled to God by the death of his Son, much more being reconciled, we shall be saved by his life" (Rom. 5:10). "If ye then being evil, know how to give good gifts unto your children, how much more shall your Father which is in heaven give good things to them that ask him?" (Mt. 7:11). So here in our text the reasoning is irresistible and goes straight to the understanding and heart.

Our text tells of the gracious character of our loving God as interpreted by the gift of His Son. This is written not merely for the instruction of our minds, but for the comfort and assurance of our hearts. The gift of His own Son is God's guarantee to His people of all needed blessings. The greater includes the less; His wonderful spiritual gift is the pledge of all needed temporal mercies. Note in our text four things:

1. *The Father's Costly Sacrifice.*

This brings before us a side of the truth on which I fear we

22

humans don't usually factor pain into planning
we sacrifice to a point
THE GREAT GIVER 23

rarely meditate. We delight to think of the Christ, whose love was stronger than death and who deemed no suffering too great to undergo for His people. But what must it have meant to the heart of the Father when His Beloved left His heavenly home! God is love, and nothing is so sensitive as love. I do not believe that Deity is emotionless, Stoic as represented by the Schoolmen of the middle ages. I believe the sending forth of His Son was something the heart of the Father felt, that it was a real sacrifice on His part.

Weigh well then the solemn fact underlying the sure promise that follows: God "spared not His own Son"! Expressive, profound, melting words! Knowing as only He could, all that redemption involved: the Law rigid and unbending, insisting on perfect obedience and demanding death for its transgressors; Justice, stern and inexorable, requiring full satisfaction, refusing to "clear the guilty." Yet God did not withhold the only suitable sacrifice.

God "spared not His own Son." Though knowing full well the humiliation and ignominy of Bethlehem's manger, the ingratitude of men, the not having where to lay His head, the hatred and opposition of the ungodly, the enmity and bruising of Satan; yet He did not hesitate. God did not relax any of the holy requirements of His throne nor abate one whit of the awful curse. No, He "spared not His own Son." The utmost farthing must be exacted; the last dregs in the cup of wrath must be drained. Even when His Beloved cried from the Garden, "if it be possible, let this cup pass from Me" (Mt. 36:29), God "spared" Him not. Even when vile hands had nailed Him to the tree, God cried "Awake, O sword, against My Shepherd, and against the man that is My Fellow, saith the Lord of Hosts; smite the Shepherd" (Zech. 13:7).

giving blood grace mercy

system guardian

Gal 3:13

redemption - bought - from who, what

marriage - united, multiply, support
family, intimacy, partner of

2. *The Father's Gracious Design.*

"But delivered him up for *us* all." Here we are told why
the Father made such a costly sacrifice; He spared not Christ
that He might spare us! It was not want of love for the Savior, but wondrous, matchless, fathomless love for us! O marvel at the wondrous design of the Most High. "God so loved
the world that he gave his only begotten Son" (Jn. 3:16).
Verily, such love passes knowledge. Moreover, He made this
costly sacrifice not grudgingly or reluctantly, but freely, out
of love.

Once God had said to rebellious Israel, "How shall I give
thee up, Ephraim?" (Hos. 11:8). Infinitely more cause had
He to say this of the Holy One, His well-beloved, the One in
whom His soul daily delighted. Yet, He "delivered Him up"
to shame and spitting, to hatred and persecution, to suffering
and death itself. And he delivered Him up for us descend-
ants of rebellious Adam, depraved and defiled, corrupt and
sinful, vile and worthless! For us who had gone into the "far
country" of alienation from Him, and there spent our sub-
stance in riotous living. Yes, "for us" who had gone astray
like sheep, each one turning to "his own way" (Is. 53:6).
For us "who were by nature the children of wrath, even as
others" (Eph. 2:3), in whom there dwelled no good thing.
For us who had rebelled against our Creator, hated his
holiness, despised His Word, broken His commandments,
resisted His Spirit. For us who richly deserved to be cast into
the everlasting burnings and receive those wages our sins so
fully earned.

Yes, for you fellow Christian, who are sometimes tempted
to interpret your afflictions as tokens of God's hardness, who
regard your poverty as a mark of His neglect, and your seasons of darkness as evidences of His desertion. O, confess to
Him now the wickedness of such dishonoring doubtings, and

grace ← common / sovereign [handwritten]

need not [handwritten]

never again question the love of Him who spared not His own Son, but delivered Him up for us all.

Faithfulness demands that I should point out the qualifying pronoun in our text. It is not God "delivered him up for all," but "for *us* all." This is definitely defined in the verses that immediately precede. In v. 31 the question is asked, "If God be for us, who can be against us?" In v. 30 this "us" is defined as those whom God did predestinate and has "called" and "justified." The "us" are the high favorites of *intimates* [handwritten] heaven, the objects of sovereign grace, God's elect. And yet in themselves they are, by nature and practice, deserving of nothing but wrath. But yet, thank God, it is "us all", the worst as well as the best, the five-hundred-pounds-debtor equally as much as the fifty-pence-debtor.

without connection to an us, even believers can suppose God is against them. [handwritten]

Calvinist [handwritten, left margin]

3. *The Spirit's Blessed Inference.*

Ponder well the glorious "conclusion" the Spirit of God here draws from the wondrous fact stated in the first part of our text, "He that spared not his own Son, but delivered him up for us all, how shall he not with him also freely give us all things." How conclusive and comforting is the inspired reasoning of the apostle. Arguing from the greater to the less, He proceeds to assure the believer of God's readiness to also freely bestow all needed blessings. The gift of His own Son, so ungrudgingly and unreservedly bestowed, is the pledge of every other needed mercy.

Here is the unfailing guaranty of perpetual reassurance to the drooping spirit of the tried believer. If God has done the greater, will He leave the less undone? Infinite love can never change. The love that spared not Christ cannot fail its objects nor begrudge any needed blessings. The sad thing is that our hearts dwell on what we have not, instead of on what we have. Therefore the Spirit of God would here still our restless thoughts and quiet the ignorant discontent with a soul-satisfying knowledge of the truth; by reminding us not only of the reality of our interest in the love of God, but also of the extent of the blessing that flows from that love.

Weigh well what is involved in the logic of this verse. First, the great Gift was given unasked; will He not bestow others for the asking? None of us supplicated God to send forth His Beloved, yet He sent Him! Now, we may come to the throne of grace and there present our requests in the virtuous and all-efficacious name of Christ.

Second, the one great Gift cost Him much; will He not then bestow the lesser gifts which cost Him nothing but the delight of giving! If a friend were to give me a valuable picture, would he begrudge the necessary paper and string to wrap it in? Or if a loved one made me a present of a precious jewel, would he refuse a little box to carry it in? How much less will He who spared not His own Son withhold any good thing from them who walk uprightly.

Third, the one Gift was bestowed when we were enemies; will not then God be gracious to us now that we have been reconciled and are His friends? If He had designs of mercy for us while we were yet in our sins, how much more will He regard us favorably now that we have been cleansed from all sin by the precious blood of His Son!

4. *The Comforting Promise*.

Observe the tense that is used here. It is not "how *has* he not with him also freely given us all things," though this is also true, for even now are we "heirs of God" (Rom. 8:17). But our text goes further than this: "How *shall* he not with Him also freely give us all things?" The second half of this wonderful verse contains more than a record of the past; it supplies reassuring confidence both for the present and future. No time limits are to be set on this "shall." Both now in the present and forever and ever in the future God shall

manifest Himself as the great Giver. Nothing for His glory
and for our good will He withhold. The same God who delivered up Christ for us all is "without variableness or
shadow of turning" (Jas. 1:17).

Mark the manner in which God gives: "How shall he not
with him also freely give us all things?" God does not have to
be coaxed; there is no reluctance in Him for us to overcome.
He is more willing to give than we are to receive. Further,
He is under no obligations to any; if He were, He would
bestow of necessity instead of giving "freely." Remember
that He has a perfect right to do with His own as He pleases.
He is free to give to whom He wills.

The word "freely" signifies not only that God is under no
constraint, but also that He makes no charge for His gifts,
He places no price on His blessings. God is no retailer of
mercies or barterer of good things; if He were, justice would
require Him to charge exactly what each blessing was worth,
and then who among the children of Adam could find the
wherewithal? No, blessed be His name, God's gifts are "without money and without price" (Is. 55:1), unmerited and un-
earned. *deny self, pick up cross, surrender, faith*

Finally, rejoice over the comprehensiveness of this *focus*
promise: "How shall he not with him also freely give us all
things?" The Holy Spirit would here regale us with the extent of God's wondrous grant. What is it you need, fellow
Christian? Is it pardon? Then has He not said, "If we confess
our sins, he is faithful and just to forgive us our sins, and to
cleanse us from all unrighteousness" (I John 1:9)? Is it
grace? Then has He not said, "God is able to make all grace
abound toward you; that ye, always having all sufficiency in
all things, may abound to every good work" (II Cor. 9:8)? Is
it a "thorn in the flesh"? this too will be given: "there was
given to me a thorn in the flesh" (II Cor. 12:7). Is it rest?
Then heed the Savior's invitation, "Come unto Me . . . and I

will give you rest" (Mt. 11:28). Is it comfort? Is He not the
God of all comfort (II Cor. 1:3)?

"How shall he not with him also freely give us all things?"
Is it temporal mercies that the reader is in need of? Are your
circumstances so adverse that you are filled with dismal fore-
bodings? Do your cruse of oil and barrel of meal look as
though they will soon be quite empty? Then spread your
need before God, and do it in simple childlike faith. Do you
think that He will bestow the greater blessings of grace and
deny the lesser ones of Providence? No, "My God shall supply all your need" (Phil. 4:19). True, He has not promised
to give all you ask, for we often ask "amiss." Mark the qualifying clause: "How shall he not with him also freely give us
all things?" We often desire things that would come in between us and Christ if they were granted, therefore God in
His faithfulness withholds them. timing, character chisels

Here then are four things that should bring comfort to every renewed heart. (1) The Father's costly sacrifice: Our
God is a giving God and no good thing does He withhold
from them who walk uprightly. (2) The Father's gracious
design: It was for us that Christ was delivered up; it was our
highest and eternal interests that He had at heart. (3) The
Spirit's infallible inference: The greater includes the less;
the best Gift guarantees the bestowment of all other needed
favors. (4) The comforting promise: Its sure foundation, its
present and future scope, its blessed extent, are for the assuring of our hearts and the peace of our minds. May the Lord
add His blessing to this meditation.

5

THE DIVINE REMEMBERER

"Who remembered us in our low estate: for His mercy endureth forever" (PSALM 136:23).

"Who remembered us." This is in striking and blessed contrast from our forgettings of Him. Like every other faculty of our beings, the memory has been affected by the Fall and bears on it the marks of depravity. This is seen from its power to retain what is worthless and the difficulty encountered to hold fast that which is good. A foolish nursery rhyme or song heard in youth is carried with us to the grave; a helpful sermon is forgotten within twenty-four hours! Most tragic and solemn of all is the ease with which we forget God and His countless mercies. But, blessed be His name, God never forgets us. He is the faithful Rememberer.

We were very much impressed when, on consulting the concordance, we found that the first five times the word "remember" is used in Scripture is in each case connected with God. "And God remembered Noah, and every living thing, and all the cattle that was with him in the ark" (Gen. 8:1). "And the bow shall be in the cloud; and I will look upon it, that I may remember the everlasting covenant between God and every living creature of all flesh that is upon the earth" (Gen. 9:16). "And it came to pass, when God destroyed the cities of the plain, that God remembered Abraham, and sent Lot out of the midst of the overthrow, when He overthrew the cities in the which Lot dwelt" (Gen. 19:29), etc. The first time it is used of man we read, "Yet did not the chief butler remember Joseph, but forgat him" (Gen. 40:23)!

The historical reference here is to the children of Israel,

when they were toiling amid the brickkilns of Egypt. Truly they were in a "low estate": a nation of slaves groaning beneath the lash of merciless taskmasters, oppressed by a godless and heartless king. But when there was no other eye to pity them, Jehovah looked on them and heard their cries of distress. He "remembered" them in their low estate. And why? Exodus 2:24, 25 tells us: "And God heard their groaning, and God remembered His covenant with Abraham, with Isaac, and with Jacob. And God looked upon the children of Israel, and God had respect unto it."

Our text is not to be limited to the literal seed of Abraham; it has reference to the whole "Israel of God" (Gal. 6:16). The saints of this present day of salvation also unite in saying, "Who remembered us in our low estate." How "low" was our "estate" by nature! As fallen creatures we lay in our misery and wretchedness, unable to deliver or help ourselves. But in wondrous grace God took pity on us. His strong arm reached down and rescued us. He came to where we lay, saw us, and had compassion on us (Lk. 10:33). Therefore each Christian can say, "He brought me up also out of an horrible pit, out of the miry clay, and set my feet upon a rock, and established my goings" (Ps. 40:2).

And why did He "remember" us? The very word "remember" tells of previous thoughts of love and mercy towards us. As it was with the children of Israel in Egypt, so it was with us in our natural ruined condition. He "remembered" His covenant, that covenant into which He had entered with our Surety from everlasting. We read in Titus 1:2 of eternal life "which God, that cannot lie, promised before the world was": i.e., He promised Christ that He would give that eternal life to those for whom our covenant Head should transact. Yes, God "remembered" that He had "chosen us in Him before the foundation of the world" (Eph. 1:4), therefore, in due time, He brought us from death to life.

Yet this blessed word goes beyond our initial experience of

God's saving grace. Historically, our text refers not only to God's remembering His people while they were in Egypt, but also while they were in the Wilderness, on their way to the Promised Land. Israel's experiences in the desert foreshadow the saints' walk through this hostile world. And Jehovah's "remembrance" of them, manifested in the daily supply of their every need, prefigures the rich provisions of His grace for us while we journey to our Home on High. Our present estate here on earth is a lowly one, for we do not now reign as kings. Yet, our God is ever mindful of us, and hourly ministers to us.

"Who remembered us in our low estate." We are not permitted to dwell on the mount always. As in the natural world, so occur our experiences. Bright and sunny days give place to dark and cloudy ones: summer is followed by winter. Disappointments, losses, afflictions, bereavements came our way, and we were brought low. And often just when we seemed to most need the comfort of friends, they failed us. Those we counted on to help, forgot us. But, even then, there was One "who remembered us" and showed Himself to be "the same yesterday and today and forever" (Heb. 13:8), and then did we prove afresh that "His mercy endureth forever" (I Chron. 16:34).

"Who remembered us in our low estate." There are some who may read these lines who will think of another application of these words: the time when you left your first love, when your heart grew cold, and your life became worldly. When you were in a sadly back-slidden state. Then, indeed, was your estate "a low" one; yet even then did our faithful God "remember" you. Yes, each of us has cause to say with the Psalmist "He restoreth my soul; He leadeth me in the paths of righteousness for His name's sake" (23:3).

"Who remembered us in our low estate." Still another application of these words may be made, and that is to the last great crisis of the saint, as he passes out of this world. As the vital spark of the body grows dim and nature fails, then too is our "estate" low. But then also the Lord remembers us, for "His mercy endureth for ever." Man's extremity is but God's opportunity. His strength is made perfect in our weakness. It is then that he "remembers" us by making good His comforting promises, "Fear thou not, for I am with thee; be not dismayed, for I am thy God; I will strengthen thee, yea, I will help thee, yea, I will uphold thee with the right hand of My righteousness" (Is. 41:10) .

"Who remembered us in our low estate." Surely this text will furnish us with suitable words to express our thanksgiving when we are at Home, present with the Lord. How we shall then praise Him for His covenant faithfulness, His matchless grace, and His loving kindness, for having "remembered us in our low estate"! Then shall we know, even as we are known. Our very memories will be renewed, perfected, and we shall "remember all the way the Lord our God hath led us" (Deut. 8:2) , recalling with gratitude and joy His faithful remembrances, acknowledging with adoration that "His mercy endureth for ever."

6

TRIED BY FIRE

"But he knoweth the way that I take: when he hath tried me I shall come forth as gold" (JOB 23:10).

Job here *corrects himself*. In the beginning of the chapter we find him saying: "Even today is my complaint bitter: my stroke is heavier than my groaning" (vv. 1, 2). Poor Job felt that his lot was unbearable. But he recovers himself. He checks his hasty outburst and revises his impetuous decision. How often we all have to correct ourselves! Only One has ever walked this earth who never had occasion to do so.

Job here *comforts himself*. He could not fathom the mysteries of Providence, but God knew the way he took. Job had diligently sought the calming presence of God for a time in vain. "Behold I go forward, but he is not there; and backward, but I cannot perceive him. On the left hand, where he doth work, but I cannot behold him" (vv. 8, 9). But he consoled himself with this blessed fact; though I cannot see God, what is a thousand times better, He can see me, "He knoweth." The One above is neither unmindful of nor indifferent to our lot. If He notices the fall of a sparrow, if He counts the hairs of our heads, of course "He knows" the way that I take.

Job here enunciates *a noble view of life*. How splendidly optimistic he was! He did not allow his afflictions to turn him into a skeptic. He did not permit the grievous trials and troubles through which he was passing to overwhelm him. He looked at the bright side of the dark cloud: God's side, hidden from sense and reason. He took a long view of life. He looked beyond the immediate "fiery trials" and said that the outcome would be gold refined. "But he knoweth the

33

way that I take: when he hath tried me I shall come forth as gold." Three great truths are expressed here: let us briefly consider each separately.

1. *The Divine Knowledge of My Life.*

"He knoweth the way that I take." The omniscience of God is one of the wondrous attributes of Deity. "For his eyes are upon the ways of man, and he seeth all his goings" (Job 34:21). "The eyes of the Lord are in every place, beholding the evil and the good" (Prov. 15:3). Spurgeon said, "One of the greatest tests of experimental religion is, What is my relationship to God's omniscience?" What is your relationship to it, dear reader? How does it affect you? Does it distress or comfort you? Do you shrink from the thought of God knowing all about your way?—perhaps, a lying, selfish, hypocritical way! To the sinner this is a terrible thought. He denies it, or if not, he seeks to forget it. But to the Christian, here is real comfort. How cheering to remember that my Father knows all about my trials, my difficulties, my sorrows, my efforts to glorify Him. Precious truth for those in Christ, harrowing thought for all out of Christ, that the way I am taking is fully known to and observed by God.

"He knoweth the way that I take." Men did not know the way Job took. He was grievously misunderstood, and for one with a sensitive temperament, to be misunderstood is a sore trial. His close friends thought he was a hypocrite. They believed he was a great sinner and being punished by God. Job knew that he was an unworthy saint, but not a hypocrite. He appealed against their censorious verdict. "*He* knoweth the way that I take: when he hath tried me I shall come forth as gold." Here is instruction for us when like circumstanced. Fellow believer, your fellow men, yes, and your fellow Christians, may misunderstand you and misinterpret God's dealings with you: but console yourself with the blessed fact that the omniscient One knows.

"He knoweth the way that I take." In the fullest sense of

the word Job himself did not know the way that he took, nor do any of us. Life is profoundly mysterious, and the passing of the years offers no solution. Nor does philosophizing help us. Human volition is a strange enigma. Consciousness bears witness that we are more than automatons. The power of choice is exercised by us in every move we make. And yet it is plain that our freedom is not absolute. There are forces brought to bear on us, both good and evil, beyond our power to resist. Both heredity and environment exercise powerful influences on us. Our surroundings and circumstances are factors that cannot be ignored. And what of providence that "shapes our destinies"? Ah, how little do we know the way we "take." Said the prophet, "O Lord I know that the way of man is not in himself; it is not in man that walketh to direct his steps" (Jer. 10:23). Here we enter the realm of mystery, and it is idle to deny it. Better far to acknowledge with the wise man, "Man's goings are of the Lord; how can a man then understand his own way?" (Prov. 20:24).

In the narrower sense of the term Job *did know* the way he took. What that "way" was he tells us in the next two verses. "My foot hath held his steps, his way have I kept, and not declined. Neither have I gone back from the commandment of his lips; I have esteemed the words of his mouth more than my necessary food" (Job 23:11, 12). The way Job chose was the best way, the scriptural way, God's way. What do you think of that way, dear reader? Was it not a grand selection? Ah, not only "patient," but wise Job! Have you made a similar choice? Can you say, "My foot hath held his steps, his way have I kept, and not declined"? (v. 11). If you can, praise Him for His enabling grace. If you cannot, confess with shame your failure to appropriate His all-sufficient grace. Get down on your knees at once, and unbosom yourself to God. Hide and keep back nothing. Remember it is written "If we confess our sins, he is faithful and just to forgive us our sins, and to cleanse us from all unrighteousness" (I John 1:9).

Does not v. 12 explain your failure, my failure, dear reader? Is it not because we have not trembled before God's commandments, and because we have so lightly esteemed His Word, that we have "declined" from His way! Then let us, even now, and daily, seek grace from on high to heed His commandments and hide His Word in our hearts.

"He knoweth the way that I take." Which way are you taking?—the Narrow Way that leads to life, or the Broad Road that leads to destruction? Make certain on this point, dear friend. Scripture declares, "So every one of us shall give account of himself to God" (Rom. 14:12). You need not be deceived or uncertain. The Lord declared, "I am The Way" (John 14:6).

2. *Divine Testing*

"When he hath tried me." "The fining pot is for silver, and the furnace for gold: but the Lord trieth the hearts" (Prov. 17:3). This was God's way with Israel of old, and it is His way with Christians now. Just before Israel entered Canaan, as Moses reviewed their history since leaving Egypt, he said, "And thou shalt remember all the way which the Lord thy God led thee these forty years in the wilderness, to humble thee, and to prove thee, and to know what was in thine heart, whether thou wouldst keep his commandments, or no" (Deut. 8:2). In the same way God tries, tests, proves, and humbles us.

"When he hath tried me." If we realized this more, we would bear up better in the hour of affliction and be more patient under suffering. The daily irritations of life, the things that annoy so much: what is their meaning? why are they permitted? Here is the answer: God is "trying" you! That is the explanation (in part, at least) of that disappointment, that crushing of your earthly hopes, that great loss; God was, is, *testing you*. God is trying your temper, your courage, your faith, your patience, your love, your fidelity.

"When he hath tried me." How frequently God's saints

see only Satan as the cause of their troubles. They regard the great enemy as responsible for their sufferings. But there is no comfort for the heart in this. We do not deny that the Devil does bring about much that harasses us. But above Satan is the Lord Almighty! The Devil cannot touch a hair of our heads without God's permission, and when he is allowed to disturb and distract us, even then it is only God using him to "try" us. Let us learn then, to look beyond all secondary causes and instruments to that One who works all things after the counsel of His own will (Eph. 1:11). This is what Job did.

In the opening chapter of Job we find Satan obtaining permission to afflict God's servant. He used the Sabeans to destroy Job's herds (v. 15), he sent the Chaldeans to slay his servants (v. 17), he caused a great wind to kill his children (v. 19). And what was Job's response? This: he exclaimed "The Lord gave, and the Lord hath taken away; blessed be the name of the Lord" (1:21). Job looked beyond the human agents, beyond Satan who employed them, to the Lord who controls all. He realized that it was the Lord trying him. We see the same thing in the New Testament. To the suffering saints at Smyrna John wrote, "Fear none of those things which thou shalt suffer; behold, the devil shall cast some of you into prison, that ye may be tried" (Rev. 2:10). Their being cast into prison was simply God "trying" them.

How much we lose by forgetting this! What a comfort for the trouble-tossed heart to know that no matter what form the testing may take, no matter what the agent that annoys, it is God who is "trying" His children. What a perfect example the Savior set us. When He was approached in the garden and Peter drew his sword and cut off the ear of Malchus, the Savior said, "The cup which My Father hath given Me, shall I not drink it?" (John 18:11). Men were about to vent their awful rage upon Him, the Serpent would bruise His heel, but He looks above and beyond them. Dear reader, no matter how bitter its contents (infinitely less than that which the Savior drained), let us accept the cup as from the Father's hand.

In some moods we are apt to question the wisdom and right of God to try us. So often we murmur at His dealings. Why should God lay such an intolerable burden on me? Why should others be spared their loved ones, and mine taken? Why should health and strength, perhaps the gift of sight, be denied me? The first answer to all such questions is, "O man, who art thou that repliest against God?" (Rom. 9:20)! It is wicked insubordination for any creature to call into question the dealings of the great Creator. "Shall the thing formed say to him that formed it, Why hast Thou made me thus?" (Rom. 9:20). How earnestly each of us needs to cry to God, that His grace may silence our rebellious lips and still the tempest within our desperately wicked hearts!

But to the humble soul who bows in submission before the sovereign dispensations of the all-wise God, Scripture reveals some light on the problem. This light may not satisfy reason, but it will bring comfort and strength when received in childlike faith and simplicity. In I Pet. 1:6 we read, "Wherein [God's salvation] ye greatly rejoice, though now for a season, if need be, ye are in heaviness through manifold temptations [or trials]: That the trial of your faith, being much more precious than of gold that perisheth, though it be tried with fire, might be found unto praise and honour and glory at the appearing of Jesus Christ." Note three things here. First, there is a necessity for the trial of faith. Since God says it, let us accept it. Second, this trying of faith is precious, far more so than gold. It is precious to God (cf. Ps. 116:15) and will yet be so to us. Third, the present trial has in view the future. Where the trial has been meekly endured and bravely borne, there will be a grand reward at the appearing of our Redeemer.

Again, in I Pet. 4:12, 13 we are told: "Beloved, think it not strange concerning the fiery trial which is to try you, as though some strange thing happened unto you: But rejoice, inasmuch as ye are partakers of Christ's sufferings: that, when his glory shall be revealed, ye may be glad also with exceeding joy." The same thoughts are expressed here as in the previous passage. There is a necessity for our "trials" and therefore we are not to think them strange; we should expect them. And, too, there is again the blessing of being richly recompensed at Christ's return. Then there is the added word that not only should we meet these trials with faith's fortitude, but we should rejoice in them, inasmuch as we are permitted to have fellowship in "the sufferings of Christ." He, too, suffered: sufficient then, for the disciple to be as his Master.

"When he hath tried me." Dear Christian reader, there are no exceptions. God had only one Son without sin, but never one without sorrow. Sooner or later, in one form or another, trial—sore and heavy—will be our lot. "And sent Timotheus our brother . . . to establish you, and comfort you concerning your faith: That no man should be moved by these afflictions; for yourselves know that we are appointed thereunto" (I Thess. 3:2, 3) . And again it is written, "We must through much tribulation enter into the kingdom of God" (Acts 14:22) . It has been so in every age. Abram was "tried," tried severely. So, too, were Joseph, Jacob, Moses, David, Daniel, the Apostles, etc.

3. *The Ultimate Issue*

"I shall come forth as gold." Observe the tense here. Job did not imagine that he was pure gold already. "I shall come forth as gold," he declared. He knew full well that there was yet much dross in him. He did not boast that he was already perfect. Far from it. In the final chapter of his book we find him saying, "I abhor myself" (42:6) . And well he might; and well may we. As we discover that in our flesh there dwells "no good thing," as we examine ourselves and our ways in the light of God's Word and behold our innumerable failures, as we think of our countless sins, both of omission and commission, we have good reason for abhoring ourselves. Ah, Christian reader, there is much dross in us. But it will not ever be thus.

"I shall come forth as gold." Job did not say, "When he hath tried me I may come forth as gold," or "I hope to come forth as gold," but with full confidence and positive assurance he declared, "I shall come forth as gold." But how did he know this? How can we be sure of the happy issue? Because the Divine purpose cannot fail. He who has begun a good work in us "will finish it" (Phil. 1:6). How can we be sure of the happy issue? Because the Divine promise is sure: "The Lord will perfect that which concerneth me" (Ps. 138:8). Then be of good cheer, tried and troubled one. The process may be unpleasant and painful, but the outcome is joyous and sure.

"I shall come forth as gold." This was said by one who knew affliction and sorrow as few men have known them. Yet despite his fiery trials he was optimistic. Let then this triumphant language be ours. "I shall come forth as gold" is not the language of carnal boasting, but the confidence of one whose mind was stayed on God. There will be no credit to our account: the glory will all belong to the Divine Refiner (James 1:12).

For the present two things are certain: first, Love is the Divine thermometer while we are in the crucible of testing: "And he shall sit [the patience of Divine grace] as a Refiner and Purifier of silver," etc. (Mal. 3:3). Second, the Lord Himself is with us in the fiery furnace, as He was with the three young Hebrews (Dan. 3:25). For the future this is sure: the most wonderful thing in heaven will not be the golden street or the golden harps, but golden souls on which is stamped the image of God; "predestinated to be conformed to the image of his Son"! Praise God for such a glorious prospect, such a victorious outcome, and such a marvelous goal.

7

DIVINE CHASTISEMENT

"Despise not thou the chastening of the Lord, nor faint when thou art rebuked of him" (HEBREWS 12:5).

It is of paramount importance that we learn to draw a sharp distinction between Divine punishment and Divine chastisement: important for maintaining the honor and glory of God, and for the peace of mind of the Christian. The distinction is very simple, yet is it often forgotten. God's people can never by any possibility be *punished* for their sins, for God has already punished them at the Cross. The Lord Jesus, our blessed substitute, suffered the full penalty for all our guilt, hence it is written "The blood of Jesus Christ his Son cleanseth us from all sin" (I Jn. 1:7). Neither the justice nor the love of God will permit Him to again exact payment for what Christ discharged to the full. The difference between *punishment* and *chastisement* does not lie in the nature of the sufferings of the afflicted: it is most important to bear this in mind. There is a threefold distinction between the two. First, let us consider the *role* God assumes in meting out either punishment or chastisement. In the former God acts as Judge, in the latter as Father. Sentence of punishment is the act of a judge, a penal sentence passed on those charged with guilt. Punishment can never fall on the child of God in this judicial sense because his guilt was all transferred to Christ: "Who his own self bear our sins in his own body on the tree" (I Pet. 2:24).

But while the believer's sins cannot be punished, while the Christian cannot be condemned (Rom. 8:33), yet he may be *chastised*. The Christian occupies an entirely different position from the non-Christian: he is a member of the family of God. The relationship that now exists between him and God is that of child and parent; and as a son he must be disciplined for wrongdoing. Folly is bound up in the hearts of all God's children, and the rod is necessary to rebuke, subdue, and humble.

The second distinction between Divine punishment and Divine chastisement lies in the *recipients* of each. The objects of the former are His enemies. The subjects of the latter are His children. As the Judge of all the earth, God will yet take vengeance on all His foes. As the Father of His family, God maintains discipline over all His children. The one is judicial, the other parental.

A third distinction is seen in the *design* of each: the one is retributive, the other remedial. The one flows from His anger, the other from His love. Divine punishment is never sent for the good of sinners, but for the honoring of God's law and the vindicating of His government. But Divine chastisement is sent for the well-being of His children: "We have had fathers of our flesh which corrected us, and we gave them reverance: shall we not much rather be in subjection unto the Father of spirits, and live? For they verily for a few days chastened us after their own pleasure; but he for our profit, that we might be partakers of his holiness" (Heb. 12:9-10).

The above distinction should at once rebuke the thoughts so generally entertained among Christians. When the believer is smarting under the rod let him not say, God is punishing me for my sins. That can never be. That is most dishonoring to the blood of Christ. God is correcting you in love, not smiting in wrath. Nor should the Christian regard the chastening of the Lord as a sort of necessary evil to which he must bow as submissively as possible. No, it proceeds from God's goodness and faithfulness, and is one of the greatest blessings for which we have to thank Him. Chastisement evidences our Divine sonship: the father of a family does not concern himself with those on the outside, but those within he guides and disciplines to make them conform to his will. Chastisement is designed for our good, to promote our highest interests. Look beyond the rod to the allwise hand that wields it!

The Hebrew Christians to whom this Epistle was first addressed were passing through a great fight of afflictions, and they were miserably conducting themselves. They were the little remnant out of the Jewish nation who had believed in their Messiah during the days of His public ministry, plus those Jews who had been converted under the preaching of the apostles. It is highly probable that they had expected the Messianic kingdom to be set up on earth and that they would be allotted the chief places of honor in it. But this had not occurred, and their own lot became increasingly bitter. They were not only hated by the Gentiles but ostracized by their unbelieving brethren, and it became a hard matter for them to make even a bare living. Providence held a frowning face. Many who had made a profession of Christianity had gone back to Judaism and were prospering temporally. As the afflictions of the believing Jews increased, they too were sorely tempted to turn their backs upon the new Faith. Had they been wrong in embracing Christianity? Was Heaven displeased because they had identified themselves with Jesus of Nazareth? Did not their suffering go to show that God no longer regarded them with favor?

Now it is most instructive and blessed to see how the Apostle met the unbelieving reasoning of their hearts. He appealed to their own Scriptures! He reminded them of an exhortation found in Proverbs 3:11-12, and applied it to their case. Notice, first, the words we place in italics: "Ye have forgotten the exhortation which speaketh *unto you.*" This shows that the exhortations of the Old Testament were not restricted to those who lived under the old covenant: they apply with equal force and directness to those of us living under the new covenant. Let us not forget that "all Scripture is given by inspiration of God and is profitable" (II Tim. 3:16). The Old Testament equally as much as the New Testament was written for our learning and admonition. Second, note the tense of the verb in our opening text: "Ye have forgotten the exhortation which speaketh." The Apostle quoted a sentence of the Word written one thousand years previously, yet he does not say "which hath spoken," but "which speaketh." The same principle is illustrated in that sevenfold "He that hath an ear, let him hear what the Spirit saith [not "said"] unto the churches" of Rev. 2 and 3. The Holy Scriptures are living words in which God is speaking today!

Consider now the words "Ye have forgotten." It was not that these Hebrew Christians were unacquainted with Prov. 3:11-12, but they had been negligent of them. They had forgotten the Fatherhood of God and their relation to Him as His dear children. In consequence they misinterpreted both the manner and design of God's present dealings with them; they viewed His dispensations not in the light of His Love, but regarded them as signs of His displeasure or as proofs of His forgetfulness. Thus, instead of cheerful submission, there was despair. Here is a most important lesson for us: we must interpret the mysterious providences of God not by reason or observation, but by the Word. How often we "forget" the exhortation that speaks to us as children: "My son, despise not thou the chastening of the Lord, nor faint when thou art rebuked of him."

Unhappily there is no word in the English language capable of doing justice to the Greek term here. *Paideia* that is rendered "chastening" is a form of *paidion* meaning "young children," the intimate word employed by the Savior in John 21:5 and Hebrews 2:13. One can see at a glance the direct connection that exists between the words "disciple" and "discipline"; equally close in Greek is the relation be-

tween "children" and "chastening." Son-training would be a
better translation. It has reference to God's education, nur-
ture and discipline of His children. It is the Father's wise
and loving correction.

Much chastisement comes by the rod in the hand of the
Father correcting His erring child. But it is a serious mistake
to confine our thoughts to this one mode. Chastisement is by
no means always the scourging of His obstinate sons. Some of
the saintliest of God's people, some of the most obedient of
His children, have been and are the greatest sufferers. Often
God's chastenings instead of being retributive are corrective.
They are sent to empty us of self-sufficiency and self-righteousness; to discover to us hidden transgressions, and to teach
us the plague of our own hearts. Or again, chastisements are
sent to strengthen our faith, to raise us to higher levels of experience, to bring us into a condition of usefulness. Still
again, Divine chastisement is sent as a preventive to subdue
pride, to save us from being unduly elated over success in
God's service. Let us consider, briefly, four diverse examples.

DAVID. In his case the rod was laid on him for grievous
sins, for open wickedness. His fall was occasioned by self-
confidence and self-righteousness. If the reader will diligently compare the two Songs of David recorded in II Sam-
uel 22 and 23, one written near the beginning of his life,
the other near the end, he will be struck by the great difference of spirit manifested by the writer in each. Read II Sam-
uel 22:22-25 and you will not be surprised that God allowed him to have such a fall. Then turn to chapter 23, and
mark the blessed change. At the beginning of v. 5 there is a
heartbroken confession of failure. In vv. 10-12 there is a
God-glorifying confession attributing victory to the Lord.
The severe scourging of David was not in vain.

JOB. Probably he tasted every kind of suffering that comes
to man: family bereavements, loss of property, grievous
bodily afflictions came fast, one on top of another. But God's

end in it all was that Job should benefit from them and be a greater partaker of His holiness. There was not a little self-satisfaction and self-righteousness in Job at the beginning. But at the end, when He was brought face to face with the thrice Holy One, he "abhorred himself" (42:6). In David's case the chastisement was retributive, in Job's corrective.

ABRAHAM. In him we see an illustration of an entirely different aspect of chastening. Most of the trials to which he was subjected were neither because of open sins nor for the correction of inward faults. Rather they were sent for the development of spiritual graces. Abraham was sorely tried in various ways in order that faith might be strengthened and that patience might have its perfect work in him. Abraham was weaned from the things of this world, that he might enjoy closer fellowship with Jehovah and become the "friend" of God.

PAUL. "And lest I should be exalted above measure through the abundance of the revelations, there was given to me a thorn in the flesh, the messenger of Satan to buffet me, lest I should be exalted above measure" (II Cor. 12:7). This "thorn" was sent not because of failure and sin, but as a preventive against pride. Note the "lest" both at the beginning and end of the verse. The result of this "thorn" was that the beloved apostle was made more conscious of his weakness. Thus, chastisement has for one of its main objects the breaking down of self-sufficiency, the bringing us to the end of ourselves.

Now in view of these widely different purposes of chastenings (retributive, corrective, educative, and preventive), how incompetent we are to diagnose, and how great is the folly of pronouncing a judgment concerning others! Let us not conclude when we see a fellow Christian under the rod of God that he is necessarily being taken to task for his sins. In the next chapter we shall consider the spirit in which Divine chastisements are to be received.

8

RECEIVING DIVINE CHASTISEMENT

*"My Son, despise not thou the chastening of the Lord,
nor faint when thou art rebuked of Him"* (HEBREWS 12:5).

Not all chastisement is sanctified to the recipients of it. Some are hardened thereby, others are crushed beneath it. Much depends on the spirit in which afflictions are received. There is no virtue in trials and troubles in themselves: it is only as they are blessed by God that the Christian is profited thereby. As Heb. 12:11 informs us, it is those who are "exercised" under God's rod who bring forth "the peaceable fruit of righteousness." A sensitive conscience and a tender heart are the needed adjuncts.

In our text the Christian is warned against two entirely different dangers: despise not, despair not. These are two extremes against which it is always necessary to keep a sharp lookout. Just as every truth of Scripture has its balancing counterpart, so has every evil its opposite. On the one hand there is a haughty spirit that laughs at the rod, a stubborn will that refuses to be humbled thereby. On the other hand, there is a fainting soul that utterly sinks beneath it and gives way to despair. Spurgeon said, "The way of righteousness is a difficult pass between two mountains of error, and the great secret of the Christian's life is to wind his way along the narrow valley."

1. *Despising the Rod.*

There are a number of ways in which Christians may "despise" God's chastenings. We mention four of them:

a. *By callousness.* To be stoical is the policy of carnal wisdom: make the best of a bad job. The man of the world knows no better plan than to grit his teeth and brave things

47

out. Having no Divine Comforter, Counselor, or Physician, he has to fall back on his own poor resources. It is inexpressibly sad when we see a child of God conducting himself as does a child of the Devil. For a Christian to defy adversities is to "despise" chastisement. Instead of hardening himself to endure stoically, he should experience a melting of his heart.

b. *By complaining.* This is what the Hebrews did in the wilderness, and there are still many murmurers in Israel's camp. A little sickness, and we become so cross that our friends are afraid to come near us. A few days in bed, and we fret and fume like a bullock unaccustomed to the yoke. We peevishly ask, Why this affliction? What have I done to deserve it? We look around with envious eyes, and are discontented because others are carrying a lighter load. Beware, my reader: it goes hard with murmurers. God always chastises twice if we are not humbled by the first. Remind yourself of how much dross is still there among the gold. View the corruptions of your own heart, and marvel that God has not smitten you twice as severely. "My Son, despise not thou the chastening of the Lord."

c. *By criticisms.* How often we question the usefulness of chastisement. As Christians we seem to have little more spiritual good sense than we had natural wisdom as children. As boys we thought that the rod was the least necessary thing in the home. It is so with the children of God. When things go as we like them or when some unexpected temporal blessing is bestowed, we have no difficulty in ascribing all to a kind Providence. But when our plans are thwarted or when losses are ours, it is very different. Yet, is it not written, "I form the light and create darkness. I make peace and create evil: I the Lord do all these things" (Is. 45:7) ?

How often is the thing formed ready to complain, "Why hast thou made me thus?" (Rom. 9:20) . We say, I cannot see how this can possibly profit my soul. If I had better health I could attend the house of prayer more frequently! If I had been spared those losses in business I would have more money for the Lord's work! What good can possibly come of this calamity? Like Jacob, we exclaim: "All these things are against me" (Gen. 42:36) . What is this but to "despise" the rod? Shall your ignorance challenge God's wisdom? Shall your shortsightedness accuse omniscience?

d. *By carelessness.* So many fail to mend their ways. The exhortation of our text is much needed by all of us. There are many who have "despised" the rod, and in consequence have not profited thereby. Many a Christian has been corrected by God, but in vain. Sickness, reverses, bereavements have come, but they have not been sanctified by prayerful self-examination.

O brothers and sisters, take heed. If God is chastening you "consider your ways" (Hag. 1:5) , "ponder the path of thy feet" (Prov. 4:26) . Be assured that there is some reason for the chastening. Many a Chrisitan would not have been chastised half so severely had he diligently inquired the cause of it.

2. *Fainting Under it.*

Having been warned against "despising" the rod, now we are admonished not to give way to despair under it. There are at least three ways in which the Christian may "faint" beneath the Lord's rebukes:

a. *When he gives up all exertion.* This is done when we sink down in despondency. The smitten one concludes that it is more than he can possibly endure. His heart fails him; darkness swallows him up, the sun of hope is eclipsed, and the voice of thanksgiving is silent. To "faint" means rendering ourselves unfit for the discharge of our duties. When a person faints, he is rendered motionless. How many Christians are ready to give up the fight when adversity enters their lives. How many are inactivated when trouble comes their way. How many, by their attitude, say, God's hand is heavy upon me: I can do nothing. Ah, beloved, "sorrow not, even as others which have no hope" (I Thess. 4:13) . "Faint not when thou art rebuked of Him." Go to the Lord about it: recognize His hand in it. Remember your afflictions are among the "all things" that work together for good.

b. *When he questions his sonship.* There are not a few Christians who, when the rod descends on them, conclude that they are not sons of God after all. They forget that it is written "Many are the afflictions of the righteous" (Ps. 34:19) , and that "we must through much tribulation enter the kingdom of God" (Acts 14:22) . One says, "But if I were His child I should not be in this poverty, misery, pain." Listen to verse 8: "But if ye be without chastisement, whereof all are partakers, then are ye bastards, and not sons." Learn, then, to look on trials as proofs of God's love; purging, pruning, purifying you. The father of a family does not concern himself much about those on the outside of his household: it is they who are within whom he guards and guides, nurtures and conforms to his will. So it is with God.

c. *When he despairs.* Some indulge the fancy that they will never get out of their trouble. One says, I have prayed and prayed, but the clouds have not lifted. Then comfort yourself with this reflection: It is always the darkest hour that precedes the dawn. Therefore, "faint not" when thou art rebuked of Him. But, says another, I have pleaded His promise, and things are no better. I thought He delivered those who called on Him; I have called, and He has not answered, and I fear He never will. What, child of God, speak of thy Father thus! You say He will never leave off smiting because He has smitten so long. Rather say He has now smitten so long I must soon be delivered. Despise not: faint not. May Divine grace preserve both writer and reader from either sinful extreme.

9

GOD'S INHERITANCE

"For the Lord's portion is his people; Jacob is the lot of his inheritance" (DEUTERONOMY 32:9).

This verse brings before us a most blessed and wonderful line of truth, so wonderful that no human mind could possibly have invented it. It speaks of the mighty God having an "inheritance," and it tells us that this inheritance is in His own people! God refused to take this world for His inheritance; it will yet be burned up. Nor did heaven, peopled with angels, satisfy His heart. In eternity past Jehovah said, by way of anticipation, "My delights were with the sons of men" (Prov. 8:31).

This is by no means the only scripture that teaches that God's inheritance is in His saints. In Ps. 135:4 we read, "For the Lord hath chosen Jacob unto Himself, and Israel for His peculiar treasure." In Mal. 3:17 the Lord speaks of His people as His "special treasure" (see margin): so "special" that the highest manifestations of His love are made to them, the richest gifts of His hand are bestowed on them, the mansions on High are prepared and reserved for them!

The same wondrous truth is taught in the New Testament. In Ephesians 1 we see the apostle Paul praying that God would give to His people the spirit of wisdom and revelation in the knowledge of Him, the eyes of their understanding being enlightened that they might know "what is the hope of His calling, and what the riches of the glory of His inheritance in the saints" (v. 18). This is a truly amazing expression; not only do the saints obtain an inheritance in God, but He also secures an inheritance in them! How overwhelming the thought that the great God should deem

Himself the richer because of our faith, love, and worship! Surely this is one of the most marvelous truths revealed in Holy Writ, that God should pick up poor sinners and make them His "inheritance"! Yet so it is.

But what need has God of us? How can we possibly enrich Him? Does He not have everything: wisdom, power, grace, glory? All true, yet there is something that He needs, yes, needs: namely, vessels. Just as the sun needs the earth on which to shine, so God needs vessels to fill; vessels through which His glory may be reflected, vessels on which the riches of His grace may be lavished.

Note that God's people are called not only His "portion," His "special treasure," but also His "inheritance." This suggests three things. First, an "inheritance" is obtained through death, so God's inheritance is secured to Him through the death of His beloved Son. Second, an "inheritance" denotes perpetuity; "to a man and his heirs forever" is a term often used. Third, an "inheritance" is for possession, it is something entered into, lived on, enjoyed. Let us now consider five things about God's inheritance:

1. *God purposed to have such an inheritance*: "Blessed is the nation whose God is the Lord; and the people whom he hath chosen for his own inheritance" (Ps. 33:12). The "nation" here is identical with the "holy nation," the "chosen generation, royal priesthood, peculiar people" of I Pet. 2:9. This favored people was chosen by God to be His inheritance: it was not an afterthought with Him, but decreed by Him in eternity past. Before the foundation of the world God set His heart on having them for Himself.

2. *God has purchased His people for an inheritance*. In Ephesians 1:14 we are told that the Holy Spirit is the "earnest of our inheritance until the redemption of the purchased possession, unto the praise of His glory." So again in Acts 20:28 we read of "the Church of God which He hath

purchased with His own blood." God has not only redeemed His people *from* bondage and death but *for* Himself.

3. *God comes and dwells in the midst of His inheritance*: "For the Lord will not cast off his people, neither will he forsake his inheritance" (Ps. 94:14), a clear proof that these scriptures are not referring to the nation of Israel after the flesh. Just as Jehovah tabernacled in the midst of the redeemed Hebrews, so He now indwells His church, both collectively and individually. "Know ye not that ye [plural] are the temple of God, and that the Spirit of God dwelleth in you?" (I Cor. 3:16). "Know ye not that your body [singular] is the temple of the Holy Spirit?" (I Cor. 6:19).

4. *God beautifies His inheritance*: Just as a man who has inherited a house or an estate takes possession of it and then makes improvements, so God is now fitting His people for Himself. He who has begun a good work within His own is now performing it until the day of Jesus Christ (Phil. 1:6). He is now conforming us to the image of His Son: each Christian can say with the Psalmist, "the Lord will perfect that which concerneth me" (Ps. 138:8). Nor will God be satisfied until we have been glorified. The Lord Jesus Christ "shall change our vile body, that it may be fashioned like unto His glorious body, according to the working whereby he is able even to subdue all things unto himself" (Phil. 3:21). "When he shall appear, we shall be like him" (I Jn. 3:2).

5. And what of the future? *God will yet possess, live on, enjoy His inheritance*. In the unending ages yet to be, God will make known the "riches of his glory" on the vessels of His mercy (Rom. 9:23). The glory that God shall ever live on—as on an inheritance—shall rise out of His people. What a marvelous statement is found at the close of Ephesians 2, where the saints are compared to a building "fitly framed together [that] groweth unto an holy temple in the Lord,"

of whom it is said, "in whom ye also are builded together for an habitation of God through the Spirit" (Eph. 2:21,22) .

A wonderful and glorious picture is presented to us in Rev. 21: "And I saw a new heaven and a new earth: for the first heaven and the first earth were passed away; and there was no more sea. And I, John, saw the holy city, the new Jerusalem, coming down from God out of heaven, prepared as a bride adorned for her husband. And I heard a great voice out of heaven saying, Behold, the tabernacle of God is with men, and he will rest in his love, he will joy over thee with singing; and God himself shall be with them, and be their God" (vv. 1-3) .

What a marvelous statement is Zeph. 3:17. "The Lord thy God in the midst of thee is mighty; he will save, he will rejoice over thee with joy; he will rest in his love, he will joy over thee with singing." The great God will yet say, "I am satisfied: here will I rest. This is Mine inheritance that I will live upon forever, even the glory which I have bestowed on redeemed sinners." Surely we have to say with the Psalmist, "Such knowledge is too wonderful for me; it is high, I cannot attain unto it" (139:6) . May Divine grace enable us to walk worthy of the vocation wherewith we are called.

10

GOD'S SECURING HIS INHERITANCE

"He found him in a desert land, and in the waste howling wilderness; he led him about. He instructed him, he kept him as the apple of his eye" (DEUTERONOMY 32:10).

In the previous verse we saw the amazing statement that the Lord's "portion" is His people, and that there may be no misunderstanding, the same truth is expressed in another form: "Jacob is the lot of his inheritance." Here in our text we learn something of the pains God takes to secure His heritage. There are four things to be noted and feasted upon.

1. *Jehovah Finding His People.*

"He found him in a desert land." It hardly needs to be said that the word "found" necessarily implies a "search." Here then we have the amazing spectacle of a seeking God! Sin came between the creature and the Creator, causing alienation and separation. Not only so, but, as the result of the Fall, every human being enters this world with a mind that is "enmity against God." Consequently, there is none that seeks after God; and thus God, in His marvelous condescension and grace, becomes the seeker.

The word "found" not only implies a search but, when we consider the sinful character and unworthiness of the objects of His search, it also tells of the love of the Seeker. The great God becomes the Seeker because He set His heart on those whom He marked out to be the recipients of His sovereign favors. God had set His heart on Abraham, and therefore sought out and found him amid the heathen idolators in Ur of Chaldea. God set His heart on Jacob, and therefore sought out and found him as a fugitive from his brother's vengeance, when he lay asleep on the bare earth. So too it was because He had loved Moses with an everlasting love that the Lord sought out and found him in Midian, at "the backside of the desert." Equally true is this with every real Christian living in the world today: "I was found of them that sought me not; I was manifest unto them that asked not after me" (Rom. 10:20).

Has God "found" you? To help you answer this question, ponder the remainder of the first part of our text: "He found him in a desert land, and in the waste howling wilderness." Is that how this world appears to you? Do you find everything under the sun only "vanity and vexation of spirit"? Are you made to groan daily at what you witness on every hand? Do you find that the world furnishes nothing to minister to the heart, let alone satisfy it? *Is* the world, really, a "waste howling wilderness" to *you?*

Let a second test be applied: when God truly "finds" one of His own He reveals Himself. He imparts to the soul a realization of His sovereign majesty, His awesome power, His ineffable holiness, His wondrous mercy. Has He thus made himself known to you? Has He given you, in any measure, a vision of His divine glory, His sovereign grace, His wondrous love? *Has* He? "This is life eternal, that they might know Thee, the only true God, and Jesus Christ, whom Thou hast sent" (Jn. 17:3).

Here is a third test: If God has revealed Himself, He has given you a sight of yourself, for in His light we "see light." A most humbling, painful, and never-to-be-forgotten experience this is. When God was revealed to Abraham, he said, "I am but dust and ashes" (Gen. 18:27). When He was revealed to Isaiah, the prophet said, "Woe is me for I am undone, because I am a man of unclean lips" (Is. 6:5). When God revealed Himself to Job, he said, "I abhor myself, and repent in dust and ashes" (Job 42:6); note, not merely I abhor my wicked ways, but my vile self. Is this your experience, my reader? Have you discovered your depravity and lost condition? Have you found there is not a single good thing in you? Have you seen yourself to be fit for and deserving only of hell? Have you, truly? Then that is good evidence, yes, it is proof positive that the Lord God has "found" you.

2. *Jehovah Leading His People.*

"He led him about." The "finding" is not the end, but only the beginning of God's dealings with His own. Having found him, He remains never more to leave him. Now that He has found His wandering child He teaches him to walk in the Narrow Way. There is a beautiful word on God's "leading" in Hos. 11:3: "I taught Ephraim also to go, taking them by their arms." Just as a fond mother takes her little ner to Christ. Have you, my reader, been brought to the Sav- one, whose feet are yet too weak and untrained to walk alone, so the Lord takes His people by their arms and leads them in the paths of righteousness for His name's sake. Such is His promise: "He will keep the feet of His saints" (I Sam. 2:9). There is a threefold "leading" of the Lord:

Evangelical. The Lord Jesus declared, "I am the way, the truth, and the life: no man cometh unto the Father but by Me" (Jn. 14:6). But again He said, "No man can come to Me, except the Father which hath sent Me draw him" (Jn. 6:44). Here then is where God leads: He leads the poor sin- ior? Is Christ your only hope? Are you trusting in the suffi- ciency of His precious blood? If so, what cause you have to praise God for having led you to His blessed Son!

Doctrinal. The Lord Jesus declared, "When He, the Spirit of truth, is come, He will guide you into all truth" (Jn. 16:13). We are not capable of discovering or entering into the Truth of ourselves, therefore we have to be guided into it. "As many as are led by the Spirit of God, they are the sons of God." (Rom. 8:14). It is He who makes us to lie down in the "green pastures" of Scripture and who leads us beside the "still waters" of His promises. How thankful we ought to be for every ray of light that has been granted us from the lamp of God's Word.

Providential. "Thou in thy manifold mercies forsookest them not in the wilderness: the pillar of the cloud departed not from them by day, to lead them in the way; neither the pillar of fire by night, to show them light and the way wherein they should go" (Neh. 9:19). Just as Jehovah led Israel of old, so today He leads us step by step through this wilderness-world. What a mercy this is. "The steps of a good man are ordered by the Lord and he delighteth in his way" (Ps. 37:23). Yes, every detail of our lives is regulated by the Most High.

> All my times are in Thy hand,
> All events at Thy command,
> All must come and last and end,
> As doth please our Heavenly Friend.

3. *God Instructing His People.*

"He instructed him." So He does us. It was to instruct us that God, in His great mercy, gave us the Scriptures. He has not left us to grope our way in darkness, but has provided us with a lamp for our feet and a light for our path. Nor are we left to our own unaided powers in the study of the Word. We are supplied with an infallible Instructor. The Holy Spirit is our teacher, "Ye have an unction from the Holy One, and ye know all things . . . the anointing ye have received of Him abideth in you, and ye need not that any man teach you" (I Jn. 2:20, 27).

Right views of God's truth are not an intellectual attainment, but a blessing bestowed on us by God. It is written, "a man can receive nothing, except it be given him from heaven" (Jn. 3:27). No matter how legibly a letter may be written, if the recipient is blind he cannot read it. So we are told, "the natural man receiveth not the things of the Spirit of God: for they are foolishness unto him: neither can he know them because they are spiritually discerned" (I Cor.

2:14). And spiritual discernment is imparted only by the Holy Spirit.

"He instructed him." How patiently God bears with our dullness! How graciously He repeats "line upon line and precept upon precept" (Is. 28:10)! Yet slow as we are, He perseveres with us, for He has promised to perfect that which concerns us (Ps. 138:8). Has He "instructed" you, my reader? Has He taught you the total depravity of man and the utter inability of the sinner to deliver himself? Has He taught you the humbling truth "Ye must be born again," and that regeneration is solely the work of God, man having *no* part or hand in it (Jn. 1:13)? Has He revealed to you the infinite value and sufficiency of the atoning sacrifice of Christ whose blood cleanses "from all sin"? Then what cause you have to be thankful for such Divine instruction.

4. *God Preserving His People.*

"He kept him as the apple of his eye" (Deut. 32:10). A religion of conditions, contingencies, and uncertainties is not Christianity; its technical name is Arminianism, and Arminianism is a daughter of Rome. It is that God-dishonoring, Scripture-repudiating, soul-destroying, system of Popery—whose father is the Devil—that prates about human merit, creature-ability, works of supererogation and a lot more blasphemous rubbish, and leaves its blinded dupes in the fogs and bogs of uncertainty. Christianity deals with certainties that originated in the purpose and love of an unchanging God, who when He begins a good work always completes it.

"For the Lord loveth judgment, and forsaketh not his saints; they are preserved forever" (Ps. 37:28). How blessed is this! Did Jehovah "forsake" Noah when he got drunk? No, indeed. Did He "forsake" Abraham when he lied to Abimelech? No, indeed. Did He "forsake" Moses for smiting the rock in anger? No, indeed, as his appearance on the Mount of Transfiguration abundantly proves. Did He "forsake" David when he committed those sins that ever since have given occasion for the enemies of the Lord to blaspheme? No, indeed. He led him to repentance, caused him to confess his awful wickedness, and then sent one of His servants to say, "The Lord hath put away thy sin" (II Sam. 12:13).

"The Lord is thy Keeper: the Lord is thy shade upon thy right hand. The sun shall not smite thee by day, nor the moon by night. The Lord shall preserve thee from all evil: he shall preserve thy soul. The Lord shall preserve thy going out and thy coming in from this time forth and even for evermore" (Ps. 121:5-8). Here are the covenant verities of our faithful God, here are the infallible "shall's" of the triune Jehovah, here are the sure promises of Him who cannot lie. Note there were no if's or peradventure's, but the unconditional and unqualified declarations of the Most High. No circumstances can ever place the believer beyond the reach of Divine preservation. No change can alter or affect this Divine certainty. Wealth may ensnare, poverty may strip, Satan may tempt, inward corruptions may annoy, but nothing can ever destroy or lead to the destruction of a single sheep of Christ; no indeed, all these things serve only to display more clearly and gloriously the preserving hand of our God.

We "are kept by the power of God through faith unto salvation ready to be revealed in the last time" (I Pet. 1:5). The rage of heathen monarchs, with their den of lions and fiery furnace, may be employed to try the faith of God's elect, but destroy them, harm them, they cannot. O brethren in Christ, what cause we have to praise the finding, leading, instructing, and preserving, Triune Jehovah!

11

MOURNING

"Blessed are they that mourn" (MATTHEW 5:4).

Mourning is hateful and irksome to poor human nature. Our spirits instinctively shrink from suffering and sadness. By nature we seek the society of the cheerful and joyous. Our text presents a dissonance to the unregenerate, yet is it sweet music to the ears of God's elect. If "blessed" why do they "mourn"? If they "mourn" how can they be "blessed"? Only the child of God has the key to this paradox. The more we ponder our text the more we are constrained to exclaim, "never man spake like this man" (Jn. 7:46) ! "Blessed [happy] are they that mourn" is at complete variance with the world's logic. Men have in all places and in all ages deemed the prosperous and gay the happy ones, but Christ pronounces happy those who are poor in spirit and who mourn.

Now it is obvious that it is not every species of mourning here referred to. There is a "sorrow of the world which worketh death" (II Cor. 2:10) . The mourning for which Christ promises comfort is spiritual. The mourning that is blessed is that which results from a realization of God's holiness and goodness and leads to a sense of our own wickedness. We mourn over the depravity of our natures, the enormity and guilt of our conduct and sorrow over our sins with a godly sorrow.

We shall consider the eight Beatitudes as arranged in four pairs. The first of the eight is the blessing that Christ pronounced on those who are poor in spirit, those who have been awakened to a sense of their own nothingness and emptiness. Now the transition from such poverty to mourning is easy to follow, in fact, it follows so closely that it is rather its companion.

The mourning here referred to is manifestly more than bereavement, affliction or loss. It is mourning for sin. "It is mourning over the felt destitution of our spiritual state, and over the iniquities that have separated between us and God; mourning over the very morality in which we have boasted, and the self-righteousness in which we have trusted; sorrow for rebellion against God, and hostility to His will; and such mourning always goes side by side with conscious poverty of spirit" (Dr. Person).

A striking illustration and exemplification of the spirit on which the Savior here pronounced His benediction is to be found in Lk. 18. Here a vivid contrast is presented. First, we are shown a self-righteous Pharisee looking up toward God and saying, "God, I thank Thee that I am not as other men are, extortioners, unjust, adulterers, or even as this publican. I fast twice in the week; I give tithes of all that I possess." This all may have been true as he looked at it, yet this man went down to his house in a state of condemnation. His fine garments were rags, his white robes were filthy, though he did not know it. Then we are shown the publican, standing afar off, who, in the language of the Psalmist was so troubled by his iniquities that he was not able to look up (Ps. 40:12). He dared not so much as lift up his eyes to Heaven, but smote his breast, conscious of the fountain of corruption within, and cried, "God be merciful to me a sinner," and that man went down to his house justified, because he was poor in spirit and mourned for sin.

Here then are the first birthmarks of the children of God. He who has never come to be poor in spirit and has never known what it is to really mourn for sin, though he belong to a church and be an officebearer in it, has neither entered nor seen the kingdom of God. How thankful the Christian reader ought to be that the great God condescends to dwell in the humble and contrite heart! Where can we find anything in all the Old Testament more precious than that? That He, in whose sight the heavens are not clean, who cannot find in any temple that man ever built for Him, however magnificent, a proper dwelling-place, has spoken Is. 66:2 and Is. 57:15 to us!

"Blessed are they that mourn." Though the primary reference is to initial mourning, usually termed "conviction of sin," it is by no means to be limited to this. Mourning is ever a characteristic of the normal Christian state. There is much that the believer has to mourn over. The plague of his own heart makes him cry, "O wretched man that I am"; the unbelief which "doth so easily beset us" and the sins which we commit that are more in number than the hairs of our head, are a continual grief; the barrenness and unprofitableness of our lives make us sigh and cry; our propensity to wander from Christ, our lack of communion with Him, the shallowness of our love for Him, cause us to hang our harps on the willows. But this is not all. The hypocritical religion prevailing on every hand, having a form of godliness but denying the power thereof; the awful dishonor done to the truth of God by the false doctrines taught in countless pulpits; the divisions among the Lord's people, the strife between brethren, occasion continual sorrow of heart. The awful wickedness in the world, men despising Christ, the untold sufferings around, make us groan within ourselves. The closer the Christian lives to God, the more he will mourn over all that dishonors Him. With the Psalmist he will say: 119:53; with Jeremiah, 13:17; 14:17; with Ezekiel, 9:4.

"They shall be comforted." This refers first of all to the removal of the conscious guilt that burdens the conscience. It finds its fulfillment in the Spirit's applying the Gospel of God's grace to the one whom He has convicted of his dire need of a Savior. It results in a recognition of free and full forgiveness through the merits of the atoning blood of Christ. This Divine comfort is the peace of God that passes all understanding filling the heart of the one who is now assured that he is "accepted in the Beloved." God wounds before He heals, abases before He exalts. First there is a rev-

elation of His justice and holiness, then the making known
of His mercy and grace.

"They shall be comforted" also receives a constant fulfillment in the experience of the Christian. Though he
mourns his excuseless failures and confesses them to God, yet
he is comforted by the assurance that the blood of Jesus
Christ His Son cleanses him from all sin. Though he groans
over the dishonor done to God on every side, yet he is comforted by the knowledge that the day is rapidly approaching
when Satan shall be removed from these scenes and when the
Lord Jesus shall sit on the throne of His glory and rule in
righteousness and peace. Though the chastening hand of the
Lord is often laid on him and though "no chastening for the
present seemeth to be joyous, but grievous" (Heb. 12:11),
nevertheless, he is consoled by the realization that this is all
working out for him "a far more exceeding and eternal
weight of glory" (II Cor. 4:17). Like the Apostle, the believer who is in communion with his Lord can say, "As sorrowful yet always rejoicing" (II Cor. 6:10). He may often
be called on to drink of the bitter waters of Marah, but God
has planted nearby a tree to sweeten them. Yes "mourning"
Christians are comforted even now by the Divine Comforter,
by the ministrations of His servants, by encouraging words
from fellow Christians, and by the precious promises of the
Word being brought home in power to their memories and
hearts.

"They shall be comforted." The best wine is reserved for
the last. Sorrow may endure for a night, but joy comes in the
morning. During the long night of His absence, the saints of
God have been called to fellowship with Him who was the
Man of Sorrows. But, blessed be God, it is written that if we
suffer with Him we shall also be glorified with Him (Rom.
8:17). What comfort and joy will be ours when shall dawn
the morning without clouds! Then shall "sorrow and sighing
flee away" (Is. 35:10). Then shall be fulfilled the saying of
Rev. 21:3-4.

12

HUNGERING

"Blessed are they which do hunger and thirst after right-eousness: for they shall be filled" (MATTHEW 5:6).

In the first three Beatitudes we witness the heart exercises of one who has been awakened by the Spirit of God. First, there is a sense of need, a realization of my nothingness and emptiness. Second, there is a judging of self, a consciousness of my guilt and sorrowing over my lost condition. Third, there is an end of seeking to justify myself before God, an abandonment of all pretences to personal merit, a taking of my place in the dust before God. Here, in the fourth, the eye of the soul is turned away from self to Another: there is a longing after what I know I have not and which I know I urgently need.

There has been much needless quibbling as to the precise import of the word "righteousness" in our present text. The best way to ascertain its significance is to go back to the Old Testament scriptures where this term is used, and then shine on these the fuller light furnished by the New Testament Epistles.

"Drop down, ye heavens, from above, and let the skies pour down righteousness: let the earth open, and let them bring forth salvation, and let righteousness spring up together; I, the Lord have created it" (Is. 45:8). The first half of this verse refers in figurative language to the advent of Christ to this earth; the second half to His resurrection, when He was "raised again for our justification" (Rom. 4:25). "Hearken unto me, ye stouthearted, that are far from righteousness: I bring near my righteousness; it shall not be far off, and my salvation shall not tarry; and I will place salvation in Zion for Israel my glory" (Is. 46:12-14). "**My righteousness** is near; my salvation is gone forth, and mine arms shall judge the people; the isles shall wait upon me, and on mine arms shall they trust" (Is. 51:5). "Thus saith the Lord, Keep ye judgment, and do justice: for my salvation is near to come, and my righteousness to be revealed" (Is. 56:1). "I will greatly rejoice in the Lord, my soul shall be joyful in my God; for he hath clothed me with the garments of salvation, he hath covered me with the robe of righteousness" (Is. 61:10). These passages make it clear that God's "righteousness" is synonymous with God's "salvation."

The above scriptures are unfolded in the Epistle to the Romans where the "Gospel" receives its fullest exposition, see 1:1. In 1:16, 17, we are told "I am not ashamed of the Gospel of Christ, for it is the power of God unto salvation to every one that believeth; to the Jew first, and also to the Greek. For therein is the righteousness of God revealed from faith to faith." In 3:22, 24 we read, "Even the righteousness of God which is by faith of Jesus Christ unto all and upon all them that believe, for there is no difference: For all have sinned, and come short of the glory of God; Being justified freely by His grace through the redemption that is in Christ Jesus." In 5:19 the blessed declaration is made, "for as by one man's disobedience many were made [legally constituted] sinners, so by the obedience of One shall many be made [legally constituted] righteous." In 10:4 we learn, "Christ is the end of the law for righteousness to every one that believeth."

The sinner is destitute of righteousness, for "there is none righteous, no not one" (Rom. 3:10). God has therefore provided in Christ a perfect righteousness for each and all of His people. This righteousness, this satisfying of all the demands of God's holy law against us, was worked out by our Substitute and Surety. This righteousness is now imputed to, legally placed to the account of, the believing sinner. Just as the sins of God's people were all transferred to Christ, so His righteousness is placed on them, see II Cor. 5:21. This then is a brief summary of the teaching of Scripture on this vital and blessed subject of righteousness.

"Blessed are they which do hunger and thirst after righteousness." Hungering and thirsting express vehement desire of which the soul is acutely conscious. First, the Holy Spirit brings before the heart the holy requirements of God. He reveals to us His perfect standard, that He can never lower. He reminds us that "Except your righteousness exceed the righteousness of the scribes and Pharisees, ye shall in no case enter the kingdom of heaven" (Mt. 5:20). Second, the trembling soul, conscious of his own abject poverty, realizing his utter inability to measure up to God's requirements, sees no help in self. This is a painful discovery, that causes him to mourn and groan. Have *you* done so? Third, the Holy Spirit now creates in the heart a deep "hunger and thirst," that causes the convicted sinner to look for relief and seek a supply outside himself. The eye is now directed to Christ, "The Lord our Righteousness" (Jer. 23:6).

Like the previous ones, this fourth Beatitude describes a dual experience, initiated and continuing that begins in the unconverted but is perpetuated in the saved sinner. There is a repeated exercise of this grace felt at varying intervals. The one who longed to be saved by Christ now yearns to be made like Him. Looked at in its widest aspect, this hungering and thirsting refers to that panting of the renewed heart after God (Ps. 42:1), that yearning for a closer walk with Him, that longing for more perfect conformity to the image of His Son. It tells of those aspirations of the new nature for Divine blessing that alone can strengthen, sustain and satisfy.

Our text presents such a paradox that it is evident no carnal mind invented it. Can one who has been brought into vital union with Him who is the Bread of Life and in whom all fullness dwells, be still found hungering and thirsting? Yes, such is the experience of the renewed heart. Mark carefully the tense of the verb: it is not "Blessed are they which *have*," but "Blessed are they which *do* hunger and thirst." Do *you*, dear reader? Or are you content with your attainments and satisfied with your condition? Hungering and thirsting after righteousness has always been the experience of God's saints: see Ps. 82:4; Phil. 3:8, 14, etc.

"They shall be filled." Like the first part of our text, this also has a double fulfillment, initial and continuous. When God creates a hunger and a thirst in the soul, He does so that He may satisfy them. When the poor sinner is made to feel his need of Christ, it is so he may be drawn to and led to embrace Him. Like the prodigal who came to his father as a penitent, the believing sinner now feeds on the One figured by the "fatted calf." He is made to exclaim "surely in the Lord have I righteousness."

"They shall be filled." Not with wine wherein is excess, but "filled with the Spirit." "Filled" with "the peace of God that passeth all understanding." "Filled" with Divine blessing to which no sorrow is added. "Filled" with praise and thanksgiving to Him who has wrought all our works in us. "Filled" with that which this poor world can neither give nor take away. "Filled" by the goodness and mercy of God, till their cup runs over. And yet, all that is enjoyed now is but a little foretaste of what God has prepared for them that love Him. In the Day to come we shall be "filled" with Divine holiness, for we shall be "like him" (I Jn. 3:2). Then shall we be done with sin forever; then shall we "hunger no more, neither thirst anymore" (Rev. 7:16).

13

HEART PURITY

"Blessed are the pure in heart; for they shall see God"
(MATTHEW 5:8).

This is another of the Beatitudes that has been grossly perverted by the enemies of the Lord; enemies who have, like their predecessors the Pharisees, posed as the champions of the truth and boasted of a sanctity superior to that confessed by the true people of God. All through this Christian era there have been poor deluded souls who have claimed an entire purification of the old man, or who have insisted that God has so completely renewed them that the carnal nature has been eradicated, so that they not only commit no sins but have no sinful desires or thoughts. But God tells us: "If we say we have no sin, we deceive ourselves, and the truth is not in us" (I Jn. 1:8). Of course such people appeal to the Scriptures in support of their vain delusion, and apply experientially verses that actually describe the legal benefits of the Atonement. "The blood of Jesus Christ His Son cleanseth us from all sin" (I Jn. 1:7) does not mean that our hearts have been washed from the corrupting defilements of evil, but that the sacrifice of Christ has availed for the judicial blotting out of sins. "Old things are passed away; behold, all things are become new" (II Cor. 5:17) refers not to our state in this world, but to the Christian's standing before God.

That purity of heart does not mean sinlessness of life is clear from the inspired record of the history of all of God's saints. Noah got drunk; Abraham equivocated; Moses disobeyed God; Job cursed the day of his birth; Elijah fled in terror from Jezebel; Peter denied Christ. Yes, perhaps someone will exclaim, But all these were before Christianity was established. True, but it has also been the same since then. Where shall we go to find a Christian of superior attainment to the apostle Paul? And what was his experience? Read Romans 7 and see. When he would do good, evil was present with him (v. 21); there was a law in his members warring against the law of his mind, and bringing him into captivity to the law of sin (v. 23). He did, with the mind, serve the law of God; nevertheless, with the flesh he served the law of sin (v. 25). Ah, Christian reader, the truth is that one of the most conclusive evidences that we do possess a pure heart is the discovery and consciousness of the impurity of the old heart dwelling side by side with the new. But let us come closer to our text.

"Blessed are the pure in heart." In seeking an interpretation of any part of this Sermon on the Mount the first thing to bear in mind is that those whom our Lord was addressing had been reared in Judaism. As said one who was deeply taught of the Spirit: "I cannot help thinking that our Lord, in using the terms before us, had a tacit reference to that character of external sanctity or purity which belonged to the Jewish people, and to that privilege of intercourse with God which was connected with that character. They were a people separated from the nations polluted with idolatry; set apart as holy to Jehovah; and, as a holy people, they were permitted to draw near to their God, the only living and true God, in the ordinances of His worship. On the possession of this character, and on the enjoyment of this privilege, the Jewish people plumed themselves.

"A higher character, however, and a higher privilege, belonged to those who should be the subjects of the Messiah's reign. They should not only be externally holy, but, 'pure in heart'; and they should not merely be allowed to approach towards the holy place, where God's honour dwelt, but they should 'see God,' be introduced into the most intimate intercourse with Him. Thus viewed, as a description of the spiritual character and privileges of the subjects of the Messiah, in contrast with the external character and privileges of the Jewish people, the passage before us is full of the most important and interesting truth." (Dr. John Brown) .

"Blessed are the pure in heart." Opinion is divided as to whether these words of Christ are to be understood literally or figuratively; whether the reference is to the new heart received at regeneration or to the moral transformation of character that results from a Divine work of grace being worked in the soul. Probably both aspects of the truth are combined here. In view of the late place which this Beatitude occupies in the series, it would appear that the purity of heart on which our Savior pronounced His blessing is that internal cleansing that accompanies and follows the new birth. Yet, inasmuch as no heart purity exists in the natural man, what is here affirmed by Christ must be traced back to regeneration itself.

The Psalmist said, "Behold Thou desirest truth in the inward parts; and in the hidden part Thou shalt make me to know wisdom" (Ps. 51:6) . How far this goes beyond the outward renovation and reformation making up such a large part of the efforts now being put forth in Christendom! Much that we see around us is a hand religion that seeks salvation by works, or a head religion that rests satisfied with an orthodox creed. But God looks on the heart, an expression that appears to include the understanding, the affections, and the will. It is because God looks within that He gives a "new heart" (Ezek. 36:26) to His own people, and "blessed" indeed are they who have received such, for it is a "pure heart."

As stated above, we believe this sixth Beatitude includes both the new heart received at regeneration and the transformation of character that follows God's work of grace in the soul. First, there is a "washing of regeneration" (Tit. 3:5) , a cleansing of the affections now set upon things above instead of things below; this is parallel with "purifying their hearts by faith" (Acts 15:9). Accompanying this is the cleansing of the conscience, "having our hearts sprinkled from an evil conscience" (Heb. 10:22), referring to the removal of the burden of conscious guilt, the inward realization that being justified by faith we "have peace with God."

But the purity of heart commended here by Christ goes further than this. What is purity? Freedom from defilement, undivided affections, sincerity and genuineness. As a quality of Christian character, we would define it as godly simplicity. It is the opposite of subtlety and duplicity. Genuine Christianity lays aside not only malice, but guile and hypocrisy. It is not enough to be pure in words and in outward deportment; purity of desires, motives, intents, are what should, and do in the main, characterize the child of God. Here then is a most important test for every professing Christian to apply to himself: Are my affections set on things above? Are my motives pure? Why do I assemble with the Lord's people: to be seen of men, or to meet with the Lord and enjoy sweet communion with Him?

"For they shall see God." Once more the promises attached to these Beatitudes have both a present and a future fulfillment. The pure in heart possess spiritual discernment and with the eyes of their understanding they obtain clear views of the Divine character and perceive the excellency of His attributes. When the eye is single the whole body is full of light. "In the truth, the faith of which purifies the heart, they 'see God'; for what is that truth but a manifestation of the glory of God in the face of Jesus Christ—an illustrious display of the combined radiance of Divine holiness and Divine benignity! . . . And he not only obtains clear and satisfactory views of the Divine character, but he enjoys intimate and delightful communion with God. He is brought very near God; God's mind becomes his mind; God's will becomes his will; and his fellowship is truly with the Father and with His Son Jesus Christ.

"They who are pure in heart 'see God' in this way, even in the present world; and in the future state their knowledge of God will become far more extensive and their fellowship with Him far more intimate; for though, when compared with the privileges of a former dispensation, even now 'as with open face we behold the glory of the Lord,' yet, in reference to the privileges of a higher economy, we yet see but 'through a glass darkly'—we 'know but in part'—we understand but in part, we enjoy but in part. But 'that which is in the part shall be done away,' and 'that which is perfect shall come.' We shall yet see face to face and know even as we are known (I Cor. 13:9-12) ; or to borrow the words of the Psalmist, we 'shall behold his face in righteousness, and shall be satisfied when we awake in his likeness' (Psa. 17:15) . Then, and not till then, will the full meaning of these words be understood 'the pure in heart shall see God.' " (Dr. John Brown) .

14

THE BEATITUDES AND CHRIST

Our meditations on the Beatitudes would not be complete unless they turned our thoughts to the person of our blessed Lord. The Beatitudes describe the character and conduct of a Christian, and as Christian character is nothing more or less than being experientially conformed to the image of God's Son, we must turn to Him for the perfect pattern. In the Lord Jesus Christ we find clearly and brightly evident the different spiritual graces found only dimly reflected in His followers. Not one or two but all of these perfections were displayed by Him, for He is not only "lovely," but "altogether lovely." May the Holy Spirit who is here to glorify Him now take the things of Christ and show them to us.

First, "Blessed are the poor in spirit." It is most blessed to see how the Scriptures speak of Him who was rich becoming poor for our sakes, that we through His poverty might be rich. Great indeed was the poverty into which He entered. Born of parents who were poor in this world's goods, He commenced His earthly life in a manger. During His youth and early manhood He toiled at the carpenter's bench. After His public ministry had begun He declared that though the foxes had their holes and the birds their nests, the Son of Man had not where to lay His head. If we trace out the Messianic utterances recorded in the Psalms by the Spirit of prophecy, we find that again and again He confessed to God His poverty of spirit: "I am poor and sorrowful" (Ps. 69:29) ; and, "Bow down Thine ear, O Jehovah, for I am poor and needy" (Ps. 86:1) ; and again, "For I am poor and needy, and My heart is wounded within me" (Ps. 109:22) .

Second, "Blessed are they that mourn." Christ was indeed the chief Mourner. Old Testament prophecy speaks of Him as "the Man of Sorrows and acquainted with grief." See Him "grieved for the hardness of their hearts" (Mk. 3:5). Behold Him "sighing" before He healed the deaf and dumb man (Mk. 7:34). See Him weeping by the graveside of Lazarus. Hear His lamentation over the beloved city, "O Jerusalem, Jerusalem . . . how often would I have gathered thy children together" (Mt. 23:37). Draw near and reverently behold Him in the gloom of Gethsemane, pouring out His petitions to the Father "with strong crying and tears" (Heb. 5:7). Bow in worshipful wonderment as you hear Him crying from the cross, "My God, My God, why hast Thou forsaken Me?" (Mk. 15:34). Hearken to His plaintive plea, "Is it nothing to you, all ye that pass by? Behold, and see if there be any sorrow like unto My sorrow" (Lam. 1:12).

Third, "Blessed are the meek." A score of examples might be drawn from the Gospels illustrating the lovely lowliness of the incarnate Lord of glory. Notice it in the men selected by Him to be His ambassadors: He chose not the wise, the learned, the great, the noble, but poor fishermen for the most part. _____ in the com_____ He kept: He sought not the rich _____ Friend of publicans and sinn_____ He performed: again and agai_____ nd tell no man what had bee_____ the unobtrusiveness of His ser_____ sounded a trumpet before th_____ ght, shunned advertising, and _____ he crowds wanted to make Him _____ m (Mk. 1:45; 7:17). When they _____ Take Him by force to make Him a king, he de_____ again into a mountain himself alone" (Jn. 6:15). When His brethren urged, "Show Thyself to the world," He declined, and went up to the feast in secret (Jn. 7). When He, in fulfillment of prophecy, presented Himself to Israel as their King, He entered Jerusalem "lowly, and riding upon an ass" (Zech. 9:9).

Fourth, "Blessed are they which do hunger and thirst after righteousness." What a summary this is of the inner life of the Man Christ Jesus! Before the Incarnation the Holy Spirit announced, "Righteousness shall be the girdle of His loins" (Is. 4:5). When He entered this world, He said, "Lo, I come to do Thy will, O God" (Heb. 10:17). As a boy of twelve He asked, "Wist ye not that I must be about My Father's business?" (Lk. 2:41). At the beginning of His public ministry He declared, "Think not that I am come to destroy the law, or the prophets: I am not come to destroy, but to ful- fill" (Mt. 5:17). To His disciples He declared, "My meat is to do the will of him that sent me" (Jn. 4:34). The Holy Spirit has said of Him; "Thou lovest righteousness, and hatest wickedness: therefore God, Thy God, hath anointed Thee with the oil of gladness above Thy fellows" (Ps. 45:7). Well may He be called "The Lord our righteousness."

Fifth, "Blessed are the merciful." In Christ we see mercy personified. It was mercy to poor lost sinners that caused the Son of God to exchange the glory of Heaven for the shame of earth. It was wondrous and matchless mercy that took Him to the Cross to be made a curse for His people. So it is "not by works of righteousness which we have done, but according to his mercy he saved us" (Tit. 3:5). He still exercises mercy to us as our "merciful and faithful High Priest" (Heb. 2:17). So also we are to be "looking for the mercy of our Lord Jesus Christ unto eternal life" (Jude 21), because He will show us mercy in "that Day" (II Tim. 1:18).

Sixth, "Blessed are the pure in heart." This too was per- fectly exemplified in Christ. He was the Lamb "without spot and without blemish". In becoming Man, He was not con- taminated, contracting none of the defilements of sin. His humanity was "holy" (Lk. 1:35). He was "holy, harmless, undefiled, separate from sinners" (Heb. 7:26). "In him was no sin" (I Jn. 3:5), therefore He "did no sin" (I Pet. 2:22) and "knew no sin" (II Cor. 5:21). "He is pure" (I Jn. 3:3).

Because He was absolutely pure in nature, His motives and actions were always pure. "I seek not Mine own glory" (Jn. 8:50) sums up the whole of His earthly career.

Seventh, "Blessed are the peacemakers." This is supremely true of our blessed Savior. He is the One who "made peace through the blood of his cross" (Col. 1:20). He was appointed to be "a propitiation" (Rom. 3:25), that is, the One who would pacify God's wrath, satisfy every demand of His broken law, and glorify His justice and holiness. So, too, He has made peace between the alienated Jew and Gentile: see Eph. 2:14-15. In a coming day He will yet make peace on this sin-cursed and war-stricken earth. When He shall sit on the throne of His father, David, then shall be fulfilled that word, "Of the increase of his government and peace, there shall be no end" (Is. 9:7). Well may He be called "The Prince of Peace."

Eighth, "Blessed are they which are persecuted for righteousness' sake." None was ever persecuted as was the Righteous One. What a word is that in Rev. 12:4! By the spirit of prophecy He declared, "I am afflicted and ready to die from my youth up" (Ps. 88:15). On His first public appearance we are told they "rose up, and thrust him out of the city, and led him unto the brow of the hill whereon their city was built, that they might cast him down headlong" (Lk. 4:29). In the temple precincts they "took up stones to cast at him" (Jn. 9:59). All through His ministry His steps were dogged by enemies. The religious leaders charged Him with having a demon (Jn. 8:38). Those who sat in the gate spoke against Him, and He was the song of the drunkards (Ps. 69:12). At His trial they plucked off His hair (Is. 50:6), spat in His face, buffeted Him, and smote Him with the palms of their hands (Mt. 26:67). After He was scourged by the soldiers and crowned with thorns, carrying His own cross, He was led to Calvary where they crucified Him. Even in His dying hours He was not left in peace, but was persecuted by revilings and scoffings. How unutterably mild in comparison is the persecution we are called on to endure for His sake!

In like manner, each of the promises attached to the Beatitudes finds its fulfillment in Christ. Poor in spirit He was, but His supremely is the kingdom. Mourn He did, yet will He be comforted as He sees of the travail of His soul. He was meekness personified, yet He will sit on a throne of glory. He hungered and thirsted after righteousness, yet now He is filled with satisfaction as He beholds His righteousness imputed to His people. Pure in heart, He sees God as no other does (Mt. 11:27). As the Peacemaker, He is acknowledged the Son of God by all the blood-bought children. As the persecuted One, His reward is great, having been given the Name above all others. May the Spirit of God occupy us more and more with Him who is fairer than the children of men.

15

AFFLICTION AND GLORY

"For our light affliction, which is but for a moment, worketh for us a far more exceeding and eternal weight of glory" (II Corinthians 4:17).

These words supply us with a reason we should not faint under trials nor be overwhelmed by misfortunes. They teach us to look at the trials of time in the light of eternity. They affirm that the present buffetings of the Christian exercise a beneficent effect on the inner man. If these truths were firmly grasped by faith they would mitigate much of the bitterness of our sorrows.

"For our light affliction, which is but for a moment, worketh for us a far more exceeding and eternal weight of glory." This verse sets forth a striking and glorious antithesis as it contrasts our future state with our present. Here a light affliction, there a mighty glory. In our affliction there is both levity and brevity. It is a light affliction and it is but for a moment but in our future glory there is solidity and eternity! To discover the preciousness of this contrast let us consider both parts in the inverse order of mention.

1. "A far more exceeding and eternal weight of glory." It is a significant thing that the Hebrew word for "glory", *kabod*, also means "weight." When weight is added to the value of gold or precious stones this increases their worth. Heaven's happiness cannot be expressed in the words of earth so figurative expressions are used to convey some aspects to us. Here in our text one term is piled on top of another. That which awaits the believer is "glory," and when we say that a thing is glorious we have reached the limits of human language to express that which is excellent and perfect. But the "glory"

awaiting us is weighted, indeed "far more exceeding" weighty than anything terrestrial and temporal. Its value defies computation; its transcendent excellency is beyond verbal description. Moreover, this wondrous glory awaiting us is not fleeting and temporal, but Divine and eternal (it could not be eternal unless it was Divine). The great and blessed God is going to give us that which is worthy of Himself, indeed that which is like Himself, infinite and ever-lasting.

2. "Our light affliction, which is but for a moment."

    a. "Affliction" is the common lot of human existence; "Man is born unto trouble as the sparks fly upward" (Job 5:7). This is part of the result of sin. It is not right that a fallen creature should be perfectly happy in his sins. The children of God are not exempted; "Through much tribulation we must enter into the kingdom of God" (Acts 14:22). God leads us to glory and immortality on a rugged road.

    b. Our affliction is "light." Afflictions are not light in themselves, often they are heavy and grievous; but they are light comparatively! They are light when compared with what we really deserve. They are light when compared with the sufferings of the Lord Jesus. But perhaps their lightness is best seen by comparing them to the glory awaiting us. As the same apostle said in another place, "For I reckon that the sufferings of this present time are not worthy to be compared with the glory which shall be revealed in us" (Rom. 8:18).

    c. "Which is but for a moment." Should our afflictions continue throughout a whole lifetime, and that life be equal in duration to Methuselah's, yet it is momentary compared with the eternity before us. At most our affliction is for this present life, a vapor that appears for a little while and then vanishes away. O that God would enable us to examine our trials in their true perspective.

3. Note now the connection between the two. Our light affliction, that is but for a moment, "worketh for us a far more

exceeding and eternal weight of glory." The present is influencing the future. It is not for us to reason and philosophize about this, but to take God at His Word and believe it. Experience, feelings, observation of others, may seem to deny this fact. Often afflictions appear only to sour us and make us more rebellious and discontented. But let us remember that afflictions are not sent by God for the purpose of purifying the flesh: they are designed for the benefit of the "new man." Moreoever, afflictions help prepare us for the glory hereafter. Affliction draws away our hearts from the love of the world; it makes us long more for the time when we shall be translated from this scene of sin and sorrow; it will enable us to appreciate by way of contrast the things God has prepared for them that love Him.

Here then is what faith is invited to do: to place in one scale the present affliction, in the other, the eternal glory. Are they worthy to be compared? No, indeed. One second of glory will more than counterbalance a whole lifetime of suffering. What are years of toil, of sickness, of battling against poverty, of persecution, even a martyr's death, when weighed over against the pleasures at God's right hand, that are for evermore! One breath of Paradise will extinguish all the adverse winds of earth. One day in the Father's House will more than balance the years we have spent in this dreary wilderness. May God grant us faith that will enable us to anticipatively lay hold of the future and live in the present enjoyment of it.

16

CONTENTMENT

"I have learned, in whatsoever state I am, therewith to be content" (Philippians 4:11).

Discontent! Was there ever a time when there was so much restlessness in the world as there is today? We very much doubt it. Despite our boasted progress, the vast increase of wealth, the time and money expended daily in pleasure, discontent is everywhere. No class is exempt. Everything is in a state of flux, and almost everybody is dissatisfied. Many even among God's own people are affected with the evil spirit of this age.

Contentment! Is such a thing realizable, or is it nothing more than a beautiful ideal, a dream of the poet? Is it attainable on earth or is it restricted to the inhabitants of heaven? If practicable here and now, may it be retained, or are a few brief moments or hours of contentment the most we may expect in this life? Such questions find answer in the words of the apostle Paul: "Not that I speak in respect of want: for I have learned, in whatsoever state I am, therewith to be content" (Phil. 4:11).

The force of the apostle's statement will be better appreciated if his condition and circumstances at the time he made it are kept in mind. When the apostle wrote (or most probably dictated) the words, he was not luxuriating in a special suite in the Emperor's palace, nor was he being entertained in some exceptional Christian household of unusual piety. Instead, he was "in bonds" (cf. Phil. 1:13, 14); "a prisoner" (Eph. 4:1), as he says in another Epistle. And yet, notwithstanding, he declared he was content!

Now, there is a vast difference between precept and practice, between the ideal and the realization. But in the case of the apostle Paul contentment was an actual experience that must have been continuous, for he says, "in whatsoever state I am." How then did Paul enter into this experience, and of what did the experience consist? The reply to the first question is to be found in the words, "I have learned . . . to be content." The apostle did not say, "I have received the baptism of the Spirit, and therefore contentment is mine." Nor did he attribute this blessing to his perfect "consecration." Equally plain is it that it was not the outcome of natural disposition or temperament. It is something he had learned in the school of Christian experience. It should be noted, too, that this statement is found in an Epistle the apostle wrote near the close of his earthly career!

From what has been pointed out it should be apparent that the contentment Paul enjoyed was not the result of congenial and comfortable surroundings. And this at once dissipates a common misconception. Most people suppose that contentment is impossible unless one can have gratified the desires of the carnal heart. A prison is the last place to which they would go if they were seeking a contented man. This much, then, is clear: contentment comes from within not without; it must be sought from God, not in creature comforts.

But let us endeavor to go a little deeper. What is "contentment"? It is the being satisfied with the sovereign dispensations of God's providence. It is the opposite of murmuring, the spirit of rebellion in which the clay says to the Potter, "Why hast Thou made me thus?" Instead of complaining about his lot, a contented man is thankful that his condition and circumstances are no worse than they are. Instead of greedily desiring more than the supply of his present need, he rejoices that God still cares for him. Such a one is "content" with what he has (Heb. 13:5).

One of the fatal hindrances to contentment is covetousness, which is a canker eating into and destroying present satisfaction. It was not, therefore, without good reason that our Lord gave the solemn commandment to his followers, "Take heed, and beware of covetousness" (Luke 12:15). Few things are more insidious. Often it poses under the fair name of thrift, or the wise safeguarding of the future, present economy so as to lay up for a "rainy day." The Scripture says, "covetousness which is idolatry" (Col. 3:5), the affection of the heart being set on material things rather than on God. The language of a covetous heart is Give! Give! The covetous man is always desirous of more, whether he has little or much. How vastly different are the words of the apostle, "And having food and raiment let us be therewith content" (I Tim. 6:8). A much needed word is that of Luke 3:14: "Be content with your wages"!

"Godliness with contentment is great gain" (I Tim. 6:6). Negatively, it delivers from worry and fretfulness, from avarice and selfishness. Positively, it leaves us free to enjoy what God has given us. What a contrast is found in the word which follows: "But they that will be [desire to be] rich fall into temptation and a snare, and into many foolish and hurtful lusts, which drown men in destruction and perdition. For the love of money is the root of all evil: which while some coveted after, they have erred from the faith, and pierced themselves through with many sorrows" (I Tim. 6:9, 10). May the Lord in His grace deliver us from the spirit of this world, and make us to be "content with such things as we have."

Contentment, then, is the product of a heart resting in God. It is the soul's enjoyment of that peace that passes all understanding. It is the outcome of my will being brought into subjection to the Divine will. It is the blessed assurance that God does all things well, and is, even now, making all things work together for my ultimate good. This experience has to be "learned" by "proving what is that good, and ac-

ceptable, and perfect, will of God" (Rom. 12:2). Contentment is possible only as we cultivate and maintain that attitude of accepting everything that enters our lives as coming
from the hand of Him who is too wise to err, and too loving
to cause one of His children a needless tear.

Let our final word be this: real contentment is possible
only by being much in the presence of the Lord Jesus. This
comes out clearly in the verses that follow our opening text;
"I know both how to be abased, and I know how to abound:
everywhere and in all things I am instructed both to be full
and to be hungry, both to abound and suffer need. I can do
all things through Christ which strengthens me" (Phil. 4:12,
13). It is only by cultivating intimacy with that One who
was never discontent that we shall be delivered from the sin
of complaining. It is only by daily fellowship with Him who
ever delighted in the Father's will that we shall learn the
secret of contentment. May both writer and reader so behold
in the mirror of the Word the glory of the Lord that we shall
be "changed into the same image from glory to glory, even as
by the Spirit of the Lord" (II Cor. 3:18).

17

PRECIOUS DEATH

"Precious in the sight of the Lord is the death of his saints" (Ps. 116:15).

This is one of the many comforting and blessed statements in Holy Scripture concerning that great event from which the flesh so much shrinks. If the Lord's people would more frequently make a prayerful and believing study of what the Word says about their departure out of this world, death would lose much if not all its terrors for them. But alas, instead of doing so, they let their imaginations run riot, give way to carnal fears, and walk by sight instead of by faith. Looking to the Holy Spirit for guidance, let us endeavor to dispel, by the light of Divine revelation, some of the gloom unbelief casts around the death of even a Christian.

"Precious in the sight of the Lord is the death of his saints." These words show that a dying saint is an object of special notice to the Lord, for note the words "in the sight of." It is true that the eyes of the Lord are always on us, for He never slumbers nor sleeps. It is true that we may say at all times "Thou God seest me." But it appears from Scripture that there are occasions when He notices and cares for us in a special manner. "God is our refuge and strength, a very present help in trouble" (Ps. 46:1). "When thou passest through the waters, I will be with thee" (Is. 43:2).

"Precious in the sight of the Lord is the death of his saints." This brings before us an aspect of death rarely considered by believers. It gives us what may be termed the Godward side of the subject. Only too often, we contemplate death, like most other things, from our side. The text tells us that from the viewpoint of Heaven the death of a saint is nei-

86

ther hideous nor horrible, tragic nor terrible, but "precious." This raises the question, Why is the death of His people precious in the sight of the Lord? What is there in the last great crisis which is so dear to Him? Without attempting an exhaustive reply, let us suggest four possible answers.

1. *Their persons are precious to the Lord.*

They ever were and always will be dear to Him. His saints! They were the ones on whom His love was set before the earth was formed or the heavens made. These are they for whose sakes He left His home on high and whom He bought with His precious blood, cheerfully laying down His life for them. These are they whose names are borne on our great High Priest's breast and engraved on the palms of His hands. They are His Father's love-gift to Him, His children, members of His body; therefore, everything that concerns them is precious in His sight. The Lord loves His people so intensely that the very hairs of their heads are numbered: the angels are sent forth to minister unto them; and because their persons are precious to the Lord so also are their deaths.

2. *Because death terminates the saint's sorrows and sufferings.*

There is a necessity for our sufferings, for through much tribulation we enter into the kingdom of God (Acts 14:22). Nevertheless, the Lord does not "afflict willingly" (Lam. 3:33). God is neither unmindful of nor indifferent to our trials and troubles. Concerning His people of old it is written, "In all their affliction he was afflicted" (Is. 63:9). "Like as a father pitieth his children, so the Lord pitieth them that fear him" (Ps. 103:13). So also are we told that our great High Priest is "touched with the feeling of our infirmities" (Heb. 4:15). Here, then, may be another reason the death of a saint is precious in the sight of the Lord: because it marks the termination of his sorrows and sufferings.

3. *Because death affords the Lord an opportunity to display His sufficiency.*

Love is never so happy as when ministering to the needs of its cherished object, and never is the Christian so needy and so helpless as in the hour of death. But man's extremity is God's opportunity. It is then that the Father says to His trembling child, "Fear thou not; for I am with thee: be not dismayed, for I am thy God: I will strengthen thee; yea, I will help thee; yea, I will uphold thee with the right hand of my righteousness" (Is. 41:10). It is because of this that the believer may confidently reply, "Yea, though I walk through the valley of the shadow of death, I will fear no evil: for Thou art with me; Thy rod and Thy staff they comfort me." Our very weakness appeals to His strength, our emergency to His sufficiency. Most blessedly is this principle illustrated in the well-known words "He shall gather the lambs [the helpless ones] with his arm, and carry them in his bosom" (Is. 40:11). Yes, His strength is made perfect in our weakness. Therefore is the death of the saints "precious" in His sight because it affords the Lord a blessed occasion for his love, grace, and power to minister to and undertake for His helpless people.

4. *Because at death the saint goes directly to the Lord.* ✓

The Lord delights in having His people with Himself. Blessedly was this evidenced all through His earthly ministry. Wherever He went, the Lord took His disciples along with Him. Whether it was to the marriage at Cana, to the holy feasts in Jerusalem, to the house of Jairus when his daughter lay dead, or to the Mount of Transfiguration, they accompanied Him. How blessed is that word in Mark 3:14, "He ordained twelve, that they should be with him." And He is "the same yesterday and today and for ever." Therefore He has assured us, "If I go and prepare a place for you, I will come again, and receive you unto Myself, that where I am, there ye may be also" (Jn. 14:3). Precious then is the death of the saints in His sight, because absent from the body we are "present with the Lord" (II Cor. 5:8). ✓

While we are sorrowing over the removal of a saint, Christ is rejoicing. His prayer was "Father, I will that they also, whom Thou hast given me, be with me where I am; that they may behold my glory" (Jn. 17:24), and in the entrance into Heaven of each one of His own people, He sees an answer to that prayer and is glad. He beholds in each one that is freed from "this body of death" another portion of the reward for His travail of soul, and He is satisfied with it. Therefore the death of His saints is precious to the Lord, for it gives Him occasion for rejoicing.

It is most interesting and instructive to trace out the full meaning of the Hebrew word here translated "precious." It is also rendered "excellent." "How excellent is Thy loving kindness, O God!" (Ps. 36:7). "A man of understanding is of an excellent spirit" (Prov. 17:27). Regardless of the worthiness or unworthiness of his life, the death of a saint is excellent in the sight of the Lord.

The same Hebrew word is also rendered "honorable." "Kings' daughters were among thy honourable women" (Ps. 45:9). So Ahasuerus asked of Haman "What shall be done unto the man whom the king delighteth to honour?" (Esther 6:6). Yes, the exchange of heaven for earth is truly honorable, and "This honour have all his saints. Praise ye the Lord."

This Hebrew word is also rendered "brightness." "If I beheld the sun when it shined, or the moon walking in brightness" (Job 31:26). Dark and gloomy though death may be to those whom the Christian leaves behind, it is brightness "in the sight of the Lord": "at evening time it shall be light" (Zech. 14:7). Precious, excellent, honorable, and bright, in the sight of the Lord is the death of His saints. May the Lord make this meditation precious to His saints.

AN INTRODUCTION TO M'CHEYNE'S
CALENDAR FOR DAILY BIBLE READING

One of the most common problems among Christians today is lack of knowledge of God's Word. This spiritual malnutrition is the cause of a stunted growth in grace, weakness in the face of temptation and persecution, and slowness to learn under affliction and chastisement. Yet God has made wonderful provision for a life of triumph in Christ. How is a life of overcoming, persevering faith to be nurtured? Such a life, filled by God with "joy and peace in believing" and based squarely upon His promises, can and will grow as it is fed a steady diet of Bible reading and memorization.

Robert Murray M'Cheyne (1813–43) was a man of God who greatly promoted the systematic reading and study of the Bible. Though he lived to be only twenty-nine and had a public ministry of less than eight years, this Scottish pastor left behind a calendar for daily Bible reading that has been a blessing to millions of believers, down to the present day. It was Mr. M'Cheyne's prayer and purpose that his congregation might willingly use this calendar for personal and family devotions. He thus took into full account the corporate nature of the Christian life, the truth that all who are "In Christ" are indeed "members one of another." This comes through clearly in his "Directions" on the use of the calendar, which are printed with it below and appropriately entitled "Daily Bread."

If families and congregations would adopt this or a similar plan, a major step would then be taken to alleviate the lack of knowledge of "the whole counsel of God" that robs so many of spiritual power and joy in the Lord. How shall Christ's Church be enabled to stand against the wiles of the devil in this evil day? We must, both individually and collectively, take upon us "the whole armor of God", especially "the sword of the Spirit, which is the Word of God."

God's Word is full of comfort for Christians, but this comfort can be appropriated only by personal knowledge of the Bible. If during peaceful days we consistently stock the pantry of our hearts with God's Word, then when trouble arrives we will surely have bread enough and to spare.

DAILY BREAD

BEING A CALENDAR FOR READING THROUGH THE WORD OF GOD IN A YEAR.

"Thy word is very pure; therefore Thy servant loveth it."

MY DEAR FLOCK,—The approach of another year stirs up within me new desires for your salvation, and for the growth of those of you who are saved. "God is my record how greatly I long after you all in the bowels of Jesus Christ." What the coming year is to bring forth, who can tell? There is plainly a weight lying on the spirits of all good men, and a looking for some strange work of judgment coming upon this land. There is need now to ask that solemn question: "If in the land of peace, wherein thou trustedst, they wearied thee, then how wilt thou do in the swelling of Jordan?"

Those believers will stand firmest who have no dependence upon self or upon creatures, but upon Jehovah our Righteousness. We must be driven more to our Bibles, and to the mercy-seat, if we are to stand in the evil day. Then we shall be able to say, like David, "The proud have had me greatly in derision, yet have I not declined from Thy law." "Princes have persecuted me without a cause, but my heart standeth in awe of Thy word."

It has long been in my mind to prepare a scheme of Scripture reading, in which as many as were made willing by God might agree, so that the whole Bible might be read once by you in the year, and all might be feeding in the same portion of the green pasture at the same time.

I am quite aware that such a plan is accompanied with many

DANGERS.

(1) *Formality.*—We are such weak creatures that any regularly returning duty is apt to degenerate into a lifeless form. The tendency of reading the word by a fixed rule may, in some minds, be to create

this skeleton religion. This is to be the peculiar sin of the last days: "Having the form of godliness, but denying the power hereof." Guard against this. Let the calendar perish rather than this rust eat up your souls.

(2) *Self-righteousness.*—Some, when they have devoted their set time to reading the word, and accomplished their prescribed portion, may be tempted to look at themselves with self-complacency. Many, I am persuaded, are living without any divine work on their soul—unpardoned and unsanctified, and ready to perish—who spend their appointed times in secret and family devotion. This is going to hell with a lie in the right hand.

(3) *Careless reading.*—Few *tremble* at the word of God. Few, in reading it, hear the voice of Jehovah, which is full of majesty. Some, by having so large a portion, may be tempted to weary of it, as Israel did of the daily manna, saying, "Our soul loatheth this light bread!" and to read it in a slight and careless manner. This would be fearfully provoking to God. Take heed lest that word be true of you: "Ye said also, Behold, what a weariness is it! and ye have snuffed at it, saith the Lord of Hosts."

(4) *A yoke too heavy to bear.*—Some may engage in reading with alacrity for a time, and afterwards feel it a burden, grievous to be borne. They may find conscience dragging them through the appointed task without any relish of the heavenly food. If this be the case with any, throw aside the fetter, and feed at liberty in the sweet garden of God. My desire is not to cast a snare upon you, but to be a helper of your joy.

If there be so many dangers, why propose such a scheme at all? To this I answer, that the best things are accompanied with danger, as the fairest flowers are often gathered in the clefts of some dangerous precipice. Let us weigh

THE ADVANTAGES.

(1) *The whole Bible will be read through in an orderly manner in the course of a year.*—The Old Testament once, the New Testament and Psalms twice. I fear many of you never read the whole Bible; and yet it is all equally divine: "All Scripture is given by inspiration of God, and is profitable for doctrine, for reproof, for correction, for instruction in righteousness, that the man of God may

be perfect." If we pass over some parts of Scripture, we shall be in-complete Christians.

(2) *Time will not be wasted in choosing what portions to read.* —Often believers are at a loss to determine towards which part of the mountains of spices they should bend their steps. Here the question will be solved at once in a very simple manner.

(3) *Parents will have a regular subject upon which to examine their children and servants.*—It is much to be desired that family worship were made more instructive than it generally is. The mere reading of the chapter is often too like water spilt on the ground. Let it be read by every member of the family beforehand, and then the meaning and application drawn out by simple question and answer. The calendar will be helpful in this. Friends, also, when they meet, will have a subject for profitable conversation in the por-tions read that day. The meaning of difficult passages may be in-quired from the more judicious and ripe Christians, and the fragrance of simpler scriptures spread abroad.

(4) *The pastor will know in what part of the pasture the flock are feeding.*—He will thus be enabled to speak more suitably to them on the Sabbath; and both pastor and elders will be able to drop a word of light and comfort in visiting from house to house, which will be more readily responded to.

(5) *The sweet bond of Christian love and unity will be strength-ened.*—We shall be often led to think of those dear brothers and sisters in the Lord, here and elsewhere, who agree to join with us in reading these portions. We shall oftener be led to agree on earth, touching something we shall ask of God. We shall pray over the same promises, mourn over the same confessions, praise God in the same songs, and be nourished by the same words of eternal life.

CALENDAR

DIRECTIONS

1. The center column (in italics) contains the day of the month. The two first columns contain the chapters to be read in the family. The two last columns contain the portions to be read in secret.

2.   The head of the family should previously read over the chapter for family worship, and mark two or three of the most prominent verses, upon which he may dwell, asking a few simple questions.

3.   Frequently the chapter named in the calendar for family reading might be read more suitably in secret; in which case the head of the family should intimate that it be read in private, and the chapter for secret reading may be used in the family.

4.   Let the conversation at family meals often turn upon the chapter read. Thus every meal will be a sacrament, being sanctified by the word and prayer.

5.   Let our secret reading prevent the dawning of the day. Let God's voice be the first we hear in the morning. Mark two or three of the richest verses, and pray over every line and word of them. Let the marks be neatly done, never so as to abuse a copy of the Bible.

6.   In meeting believers on the street or elsewhere, when an easy opportunity offers, recur to the chapters read that morning. This will be a blessed exchange for those *idle words* which waste the soul and grieve the Holy Spirit of God. In writing letters to those at a distance, make use of the provision that day gathered.

7.   Above all, use the word as a lamp to your feet and a light to your path—your guide in perplexity, your armour in temptation, your food in times of faintness. Hear the constant cry of the great Intercessor,

"SANCTIFY THEM THROUGH THY TRUTH: THY WORD
IS TRUTH."

Robert Murray M'Cheyne
St. Peter's, Dundee, Scotland, December 30, 1842.

JANUARY

THIS IS MY BELOVED SON, IN WHOM I AM WELL PLEASED. HEAR YE HIM.

FAMILY				SECRET			
GENESIS	1	MATTHEW	1	*1*	EZRA	1	ACTS	1
,,	2	,,	2	*2*	,,	2	,,	2
,,	3	,,	3	*3*	,,	3	,,	3
,,	4	,,	4	*4*	,,	4	,,	4
,,	5	,,	5	*5*	,,	5	,,	5
,,	6	,,	6	*6*	,,	6	,,	6
,,	7	,,	7	*7*	,,	7	,,	7
,,	8	,,	8	*8*	,,	8	,,	8
,,	9-10	,,	9	*9*	,,	9	,,	9
,,	11	,,	10	*10*	,,	10	,,	10
,,	12	,,	11	*11*	NEHEMIAH	1	,,	11
,,	13	,,	12	*12*	,,	2	,,	12
,,	14	,,	13	*13*	,,	3	,,	13
,,	15	,,	14	*14*	,,	4	,,	14
,,	16	,,	15	*15*	,,	5	,,	15
,,	17	,,	16	*16*	,,	6	,,	16
,,	18	,,	17	*17*	,,	7	,,	17
,,	19	,,	18	*18*	,,	8	,,	18
,,	20	,,	19	*19*	,,	9	,,	19
,,	21	,,	20	*20*	,,	10	,,	20
,,	22	,,	21	*21*	,,	11	,,	21
,,	23	,,	22	*22*	,,	12	,,	22
,,	24	,,	23	*23*	,,	13	,,	23
,,	25	,,	24	*24*	ESTHER	1	,,	24
,,	26	,,	25	*25*	,,	2	,,	25
,,	27	,,	26	*26*	,,	3	,,	26
,,	28	,,	27	*27*	,,	4	,,	27
,,	29	,,	28	*28*	,,	5	,,	28
,,	30	MARK	1	*29*	,,	6	ROMANS	1
,,	31	,,	2	*30*	,,	7	,,	2
,,	32	,,	3	*31*	,,	8	,,	3

FEBRUARY

I HAVE ESTEEMED THE WORDS OF HIS MOUTH MORE THAN
MY NECESSARY FOOD.

FAMILY					SECRET			
GENESIS	33	MARK	4	*1*	ESTHER 9-10		ROMANS	4
,,	34	,,	5	*2*	JOB	1	,,	5
,,	35-36	,,	6	*3*	,,	2	,,	6
,,	37	,,	7	*4*	,,	3	,,	7
,,	38	,,	8	*5*	,,	4	,,	8
,,	39	,,	9	*6*	,,	5	,,	9
,,	40	,,	10	7	,,	6	,,	10
,,	41	,,	11	*8*	,,	7	,,	11
,,	42	,,	12	*9*	,,	8	,,	12
,,	43	,,	13	*10*	,,	9	,,	13
,,	44	,,	14	*11*	,,	10	,,	14
,,	45	,,	15	*12*	,,	11	,,	15
,,	46	,,	16	*13*	,,	12	,,	16
,,	47	LK. 1 to v. 38		*14*	,,	13	1 COR.	1
,,	48	,,	1 v. 39	*15*	,,	14	,,	2
,,	49	,,	2	*16*	,,	15	,,	3
,,	50	,,	3	*17*	,,	16-17	,,	4
EXODUS	1	,,	4	*18*	,,	18	,,	5
,,	2	,,	5	*19*	,,	19	,,	6
,,	3	,,	6	*20*	,,	20	,,	7
,,	4	,,	7	*21*	,,	21	,,	8
,,	5	,,	8	*22*	,,	22	,,	9
,,	6	,,	9	*23*	,,	23	,,	10
,,	7	,,	10	*24*	,,	24	,,	11
,,	8	,,	11	*25*	,,	25-26	,,	12
,,	9	,,	12	*26*	,,	27	,,	13
,,	10	,,	13	*27*	,,	28	,,	14
11-12 to v. 21		,,	14	*28*	,,	29	,,	15

MARCH

MARY KEPT ALL THESE THINGS, AND PONDERED
THEM IN HER HEART.

FAMILY				SECRET			
Ex. 12 v. 22	Luke	15	*1*	Job	30	1 Cor.	16
,,	13	,,	16	*2*	,,	31	2 Cor.	1
,,	14	,,	17	*3*	,,	32	,,	2
,,	15	,,	18	*4*	,,	33	,,	3
,,	16	,,	19	*5*	,,	34	,,	4
,,	17	,,	20	*6*	,,	35	,,	5
,,	18	,,	21	*7*	,,	36	,,	6
,,	19	,,	22	*8*	,,	37	,,	7
,,	20	,,	23	*9*	,,	38	,,	8
,,	21	,,	24	*10*	,,	39	,,	9
,,	22	John	1	*11*	,,	40	,,	10
,,	23	,,	2	*12*	,,	41	,,	11
,,	24	,,	3	*13*	,,	42	,,	12
,,	25	,,	4	*14*	Prov.	1	,,	13
,,	26	,,	5	*15*	,,	2	Gal.	1
,,	27	,,	6	*16*	,,	3	,,	2
,,	28	,,	7	*17*	,,	4	,,	3
,,	29	,,	8	*18*	,,	5	,,	4
,,	30	,,	9	*19*	,,	6	,,	5
,,	31	,,	10	*20*	,,	7	,,	6
,,	32	,,	11	*21*	,,	8	Eph.	1
,,	33	,,	12	*22*	,,	9	,,	2
,,	34	,,	13	*23*	,,	10	,,	3
,,	35	,,	14	*24*	,,	11	,,	4
,,	36	,,	15	*25*	,,	12	,,	5
,,	37	,,	16	*26*	,,	13	,,	6
,,	38	,,	17	*27*	,,	14	Phil.	1
,,	39	,,	18	*28*	,,	15	,,	2
,,	40	,,	19	*29*	,,	16	,,	3
Lev.	1	,,	20	*30*	,,	17	,,	4
,,	2-3	,,	21	*31*	,,	18	Col.	1

APRIL

**O SEND OUT THY LIGHT AND THY TRUTH: LET THEM
LEAD ME.**

FAMILY					SECRET			
Lev.	4	Psalms	1-2	1	Prov.	19	Col.	2
,,	5	,,	3-4	2	,,	20	,,	3
,,	6	,,	5-6	3	,,	21	,,	4
,,	7	,,	7-8	4	,,	22	1 Thess.	1
,,	8	,,	9	5	,,	23	,,	2
,,	9	,,	10	6	,,	24	,,	3
,,	10	,,	11-12	7	,,	25	,,	4
,,	11-12	,,	13-14	8	,,	26	,,	5
,,	13	,,	15-16	9	,,	27	2 Thess.	1
,,	14	,,	17	10	,,	28	,,	2
,,	15	,,	18	11	,,	29	,,	3
,,	16	,,	19	12	,,	30	1 Tim.	1
,,	17	,,	20-21	13	,,	31	,,	2
,,	18	,,	22	14	Eccles.	1	,,	3
,,	19	,,	23-24	15	,,	2	,,	4
,,	20	,,	25	16	,,	3	,,	5
,,	21	,,	26-27	17	,,	4	,,	6
,,	22	,,	28-29	18	,,	5	2 Tim.	1
,,	23	,,	30	19	,,	6	,,	2
,,	24	,,	31	20	,,	7	,,	3
,,	25	,,	32	21	,,	8	,,	4
,,	26	,,	33	22	,,	9	Titus	1
,,	27	,,	34	23	,,	10	,,	2
Num.	1	,,	35	24	,,	11	,,	3
,,	2	,,	36	25	,,	12	Philem.	1
,,	3	,,	37	26	Song	1	Heb.	1
,,	4	,,	38	27	,,	2	,,	2
,,	5	,,	39	28	,,	3	,,	3
,,	6	,,	40-41	29	,,	4	,,	4
,,	7	,,	42-43	30	,,	5	,,	5

MAY

FROM A CHILD THOU HAST KNOWN THE SCRIPTURES.

FAMILY				SECRET			
NUMBERS	8	PSALMS	44	*1*	SONG	6	HEBREWS	6
,,	9	,,	45	*2*	,,	7	,,	7
,,	10	,,	46-47	*3*	,,	8	,,	8
,,	11	,,	48	*4*	ISAIAH	1	,,	9
,,	12-13	,,	49	*5*	,,	2	,,	10
,,	14	,,	50	*6*	,,	3-4	,,	11
,,	15	,,	51	*7*	,,	5	,,	12
,,	16	,,	52-54	*8*	,,	6	,,	13
,,	17-18	,,	55	*9*	,,	7	JAMES	1
,,	19	,,	56-57	*10*	8-9 to v. 7		,,	2
,,	20	,,	58-59	*11*	9 v. 8, 10 v. 4		,,	3
,,	21	,,	60-61	*12*	,,	10 v. 5	,,	4
,,	22	,,	62-63	*13*	,,	11-12	,,	5
,,	23	,,	64-65	*14*	,,	13	1 PETER	1
,,	24	,,	66-67	*15*	,,	14	,,	2
,,	25	,,	68	*16*	,,	15	,,	3
,,	26	,,	69	*17*	,,	16	,,	4
,,	27	,,	70-71	*18*	,,	17-18	,,	5
,,	28	,,	72	*19*	,,	19-20	2 PETER	1
,,	29	,,	73	*20*	,,	21	,,	2
,,	30	,,	74	*21*	,,	22	,,	3
,,	31	,,	75-76	*22*	,,	23	1 JOHN	1
,,	32	,,	77	*23*	,,	24	,,	2
,,	33	78 to v. 37		*24*	,,	25	,,	3
,,	34	78 v. 38		*25*	,,	26	,,	4
,,	35	,,	79	*26*	,,	27	,,	5
,,	36	,,	80	*27*	,,	28	2 JOHN	1
DEUT.	1	,,	81-82	*28*	,,	29	3 JOHN	1
,,	2	,,	83-84	*29*	,,	30	JUDE	1
,,	3	,,	85	*30*	,,	31	REV.	1
,,	4	,,	86-87	*31*	,,	32	,,	2

JUNE

BLESSED IS HE THAT READETH AND THEY THAT HEAR.

FAMILY				SECRET			
DEUT.	5	PSALMS	88	*1*	ISAIAH	33	REV.	3
"	6	"	89	*2*	"	34	"	4
"	7	"	90	*3*	"	35	"	5
"	8	"	91	*4*	"	36	"	6
"	9	"	92-93	*5*	"	37	"	7
"	10	"	94	*6*	"	38	"	8
"	11	"	95-96	*7*	"	39	"	9
"	12	"	97-98	*8*	"	40	"	10
"	13-14	"	99-101	*9*	"	41	"	11
"	15	"	102	*10*	"	42	"	12
"	16	"	103	*11*	"	43	"	13
"	17	"	104	*12*	"	44	"	14
"	18	"	105	*13*	"	45	"	15
"	19	"	106	*14*	"	46	"	16
"	20	"	107	*15*	"	47	"	17
"	21	" 108-109		*16*	"	48	"	18
"	22	" 110-111		*17*	"	49	"	19
"	23	" 112-113		*18*	"	50	"	20
"	24	" 114-115		*19*	"	51	"	21
"	25	"	116	*20*	"	52	"	22
"	26	" 117-118		*21*	"	53	MATT.	1
27-28 to v. 19		119 to v. 24		*22*	"	54	"	2
28 v. 20		v. 25 to 48		*23*	"	55	"	3
"	29	v. 49 to 72		*24*	"	56	"	4
"	30	v. 73 to 96		*25*	"	57	"	5
"	31	v. 97 to 120		*26*	"	58	"	6
"	32	v. 121 to 144		*27*	"	59	"	7
"	33-34	v. 145 to 176		*28*	"	60	"	8
JOSHUA	1	" 120-122		*29*	"	61	"	9
"	2	" 123-125		*30*	"	62	"	10

JULY

THEY RECEIVED THE WORD WITH ALL READINESS OF MIND, AND SEARCHED THE SCRIPTURES DAILY.

FAMILY				SECRET			
Joshua	3	Ps. 126-128	*1*	Isaiah	63	Matt.	11
"	4	" 129-131	*2*	"	64	"	12
5-6 to v. 5		" 132-134	*3*	"	65	"	13
6 v. 6		" 135-136	*4*	"	66	"	14
"	7	" 137-138	*5*	Jer.	1	"	15
"	8	" 139	*6*	"	2	"	16
"	9	" 140-141	*7*	"	3	"	17
"	10	" 142-143	*8*	"	4	"	18
"	11	" 144	*9*	"	5	"	19
"	12-13	" 145	*10*	"	6	"	20
"	14-15	" 146-147	*11*	"	7	"	21
"	16-17	" 148	*12*	"	8	"	22
"	18-19	" 149-150	*13*	"	9	"	23
"	20-21	Acts 1	*14*	"	10	"	24
"	22	" 2	*15*	"	11	"	25
"	23	" 3	*16*	"	12	"	26
"	24	" 4	*17*	"	13	"	27
Judges	1	" 5	*18*	"	14	"	28
"	2	" 6	*19*	"	15	Mark	1
"	3	" 7	*20*	"	16	"	2
"	4	" 8	*21*	"	17	"	3
"	5	" 9	*22*	"	18	"	4
"	6	" 10	*23*	"	19	"	5
"	7	" 11	*24*	"	20	"	6
"	8	" 12	*25*	"	21	"	7
"	9	" 13	*26*	"	22	"	8
10-11 to v. 11		" 14	*27*	"	23	"	9
11 v. 12		" 15	*28*	"	24	"	10
"	12	" 16	*29*	"	25	"	11
"	13	" 17	*30*	"	26	"	12
"	14	" 18	*31*	"	27	"	13

AUGUST

SPEAK, LORD! FOR THY SERVANT
HEARETH.

FAMILY					SECRET			
JUDGES	15	ACTS	19	*1*	JER.	28	MARK	14
"	16	"	20	*2*	"	29	"	15
"	17	"	21	*3*	"	30-31	"	16
"	18	"	22	*4*	"	32	PSALMS	1-2
"	19	"	23	*5*	"	33	"	3-4
"	20	"	24	*6*	"	34	"	5-6
"	21	"	25	*7*	"	35	"	7-8
RUTH	1	"	26	*8*	"	36, 45	"	9
"	2	"	27	*9*	"	37	"	10
"	3-4	"	28	*10*	"	38	"	11-12
1 SAM.	1	ROMANS	1	*11*	"	39	"	13-14
"	2	"	2	*12*	"	40	"	15-16
"	3	"	3	*13*	"	41	"	17
"	4	"	4	*14*	"	42	"	18
"	5-6	"	5	*15*	"	43	"	19
"	7-8	"	6	*16*	"	44	"	20-21
"	9	"	7	*17*	"	46	"	22
"	10	"	8	*18*	"	47	"	23-24
"	11	"	9	*19*	"	48	"	25
"	12	"	10	*20*	"	49	"	26-27
"	13	"	11	*21*	"	50	"	28-29
"	14	"	12	*22*	"	51	"	30
"	15	"	13	*23*	"	52	"	31
"	16	"	14	*24*	LAMEN.	1	"	32
"	17	"	15	*25*	"	2	"	33
"	18	"	16	*26*	"	3	"	34
"	19	1 COR.	1	*27*	"	4	"	35
"	20	"	2	*28*	"	5	"	36
"	21-22	"	3	*29*	EZEKIEL	1	"	37
"	23	"	4	*30*	"	2	"	38
"	24	"	5	*31*	"	3	"	39

SEPTEMBER

THE LAW OF THE LORD IS PERFECT, CONVERTING
THE SOUL.

FAMILY					SECRET			
1 Sam.	25	1 Cor.	6	*1*	Ezek.	4	Ps.	40-41
,,	26	,,	7	*2*	,,	5	,,	42-43
,,	27	,,	8	*3*	,,	6	,,	44
,,	28	,,	9	*4*	,,	7	,,	45
,,	29-30	,,	10	*5*	,,	8	,,	46-47
,,	31	,,	11	*6*	,,	9	,,	48
2 Sam.	1	,,	12	*7*	,,	10	,,	49
,,	2	,,	13	*8*	,,	11	,,	50
,,	3	,,	14	*9*	,,	12	,,	51
,,	4-5	,,	15	*10*	,,	13	,,	52-54
,,	6	,,	16	*11*	,,	14	,,	55
,,	7	2 Cor.	1	*12*	,,	15	,,	56-57
,,	8-9	,,	2	*13*	,,	16	,,	58-59
,,	10	,,	3	*14*	,,	17	,,	60-61
,,	11	,,	4	*15*	,,	18	,,	62-63
,,	12	,,	5	*16*	,,	19	,,	64-65
,,	13	,,	6	*17*	,,	20	,,	66-67
,,	14	,,	7	*18*	,,	21	,,	68
,,	15	,,	8	*19*	,,	22	,,	69
,,	16	,,	9	*20*	,,	23	,,	70-71
,,	17	,,	10	*21*	,,	24	,,	72
,,	18	,,	11	*22*	,,	25	,,	73
,,	19	,,	12	*23*	,,	26	,,	74
,,	20	,,	13	*24*	,,	27	,,	75-76
,,	21	Gal.	1	*25*	,,	28	,,	77
,,	22	,,	2	*26*	,,	29		78 to v. 37
,,	23	,,	3	*27*	,,	30		78 v. 38
,,	24	,,	4	*28*	,,	31	,,	79
1 Kings	1	,,	5	*29*	,,	32	,,	80
,,	2	,,	6	*30*	,,	33	,,	81-82

OCTOBER

O HOW I LOVE THY LAW! IT IS MY MEDITATION
ALL THE DAY.

FAMILY					SECRET			
1 KINGS	3	EPH.	1	*1*	EZEK.	34	PS.	83-84
,,	4-5	,,	2	*2*	,,	35	,,	85
,,	6	,,	3	*3*	,,	36	,,	86
,,	7	,,	4	*4*	,,	37	,,	87-88
,,	8	,,	5	*5*	,,	38	,,	89
,,	9	,,	6	*6*	,,	39	,,	90
,,	10	PHIL.	1	*7*	,,	40	,,	91
,,	11	,,	2	*8*	,,	41	,,	92-93
,,	12	,,	3	*9*	,,	42	,,	94
,,	13	,,	4	*10*	,,	43	,,	95-96
,,	14	COL.	1	*11*	,,	44	,,	97-98
,,	15	,,	2	*12*	,,	45	,,	99-101
,,	16	,,	3	*13*	,,	46	,,	102
,,	17	,,	4	*14*	,,	47	,,	103
,,	18	1 THESS.	1	*15*	,,	48	,,	104
,,	19	,,	2	*16*	DAN.	1	,,	105
,,	20	,,	3	*17*	,,	2	,,	106
,,	21	,,	4	*18*	,,	3	,,	107
,,	22	,,	5	*19*	,,	4	,, 108-109	
2 KINGS	1	2 THESS.	1	*20*	,,	5	,, 110-111	
,,	2	,,	2	*21*	,,	6	,, 112-113	
,,	3	,,	3	*22*	,,	7	,, 114-115	
,,	4	1 TIM.	1	*23*	,,	8	,,	116
,,	5	,,	2	*24*	,,	9	,, 117-118	
,,	6	,,	3	*25*	,,	10	119 to v. 24	
,,	7	,,	4	*26*	,,	11	v. 25 to 48	
,,	8	,,	5	*27*	,,	12	v. 49 to 72	
,,	9	,,	6	*28*	HOSEA	1	v. 73 to 96	
,,	10-11	2 TIM.	1	*29*	,,	2	v. 97 to 120	
,,	12	,,	2	*30*	,,	3-4	v. 121 to 144	
,,	13	,,	3	*31*	,,	5-6	v. 145 to 176	

NOVEMBER

AS NEW-BORN BABES, DESIRE THE SINCERE MILK OF THE
WORD, THAT YE MAY GROW THEREBY.

FAMILY					SECRET			
2 KINGS	14	2 TIM.	4	1	HOSEA	7	Ps.	120-122
,,	15	TITUS	1	2	,,	8	,,	123-125
,,	16	,,	2	3	,,	9	,,	126-128
,,	17	,,	3	4	,,	10	,,	129-131
,,	18	PHILEM.	1	5	,,	11	,,	132-134
,,	19	HEB.	1	6	,,	12	,,	135-136
,,	20	,,	2	7	,,	13	,,	137-138
,,	21	,,	3	8	,,	14	,,	139
,,	22	,,	4	9	JOEL	1	,,	140-141
,,	23	,,	5	10	,,	2	,,	142
,,	24	,,	6	11	,,	3	,,	143
,,	25	,,	7	12	AMOS	1	,,	144
1 CHR.	1-2	,,	8	13	,,	2	,,	145
,,	3-4	,,	9	14	,,	3	,,	146-147
,,	5-6	,,	10	15	,,	4	,,	148-150
,,	7-8	,,	11	16	,,	5	Lk.	1 to v. 38
,,	9-10	,,	12	17	,,	6	,,	1 v. 39
,,	11-12	,,	13	18	,,	7	,,	2
,,	13-14	JAMES	1	19	,,	8	,,	3
,,	15	,,	2	20	,,	9	,,	4
,,	16	,,	3	21	OBADIAH	1	,,	5
,,	17	,,	4	22	JONAH	1	,,	6
,,	18	,,	5	23	,,	2	,,	7
,,	19-20	1 PETER	1	24	,,	3	,,	8
,,	21	,,	2	25	,,	4	,,	9
,,	22	,,	3	26	MICAH	1	,,	10
,,	23	,,	4	27	,,	2	,,	11
,,	24-25	,,	5	28	,,	3	,,	12
,,	26-27	2 PETER	1	29	,,	4	,,	13
,,	28	,,	2	30	,,	5	,,	14

DECEMBER

THE LAW OF HIS GOD IS IN HIS HEART; NONE OF
HIS STEPS SHALL SLIDE.

FAMILY					SECRET			
1 CHR.	29	2 PETER	3	*1*	MICAH	6	LUKE	15
2 CHR.	1	1 JOHN	1	*2*	"	7	"	16
"	2	"	2	*3*	NAHUM	1	"	17
"	3-4	"	3	*4*	"	2	"	18
5-6 to v. 11		"	4	*5*	"	3	"	19
6 v. 12		"	5	*6*	HAB.	1	"	20
"	7	2 JOHN	1	*7*	"	2	"	21
"	8	3 JOHN	1	*8*	"	3	"	22
"	9	JUDE	1	*9*	ZEPH.	1	"	23
"	10	REV.	1	*10*	"	2	"	24
"	11-12	"	2	*11*	"	3	JOHN	1
"	13	"	3	*12*	HAGGAI	1	"	2
"	14-15	"	4	*13*	"	2	"	3
"	16	"	5	*14*	ZECH.	1	"	4
"	17	"	6	*15*	"	2	"	5
"	18	"	7	*16*	"	3	"	6
"	19-20	"	8	*17*	"	4	"	7
"	21	"	9	*18*	"	5	"	8
"	22-23	"	10	*19*	"	6	"	9
"	24	"	11	*20*	"	7	"	10
"	25	"	12	*21*	"	8	"	11
"	26	"	13	*22*	"	9	"	12
"	27-28	"	14	*23*	"	10	"	13
"	29	"	15	*24*	"	11	"	14
"	30	"	16	*25*	12-13 to v. 1		"	15
"	31	"	17	*26*	13 v. 2		"	16
"	32	"	18	*27*	"	14	"	17
"	33	"	19	*28*	MAL.	1	"	18
"	34	"	20	*29*	"	2	"	19
"	35	"	21	*30*	"	3	"	20
"	36	"	22	*31*	"	4	"	21

DATE	HOW GOD ANSWERED	MY PRAYER REQUEST	DATE

DATE	HOW GOD ANSWERED	MY PRAYER REQUEST	DATE

DATE	MY PRAYER REQUEST	HOW GOD ANSWERED	DATE

DATE	HOW GOD ANSWERED	MY PRAYER REQUEST	DATE

DATE	MY PRAYER REQUEST	HOW GOD ANSWERED	DATE

DATE	HOW GOD ANSWERED	MY PRAYER REQUEST	DATE